THE HUMAN STORM!

By
Nicson Lebrun

Copyright © Nicson Lebrun (2024)
All rights are reserved. No part of this publication will be reproduced, stored in a retrieval system, or transmitted in any form or by any means, electronic, mechanical, photocopying, recording, or otherwise, without prior permission of the author.

ISBN:
978-1-917116-39-8 (Paperback)
978-1-917116-39-8 (Hardcover)

Dedications:

This book is dedicated to all women, especially to the wife of my love, Yannie. Their Feminine veil and its kaleidoscopic manifestation that has been deployed all over my soul all along this journey from start to finish.

Acknowledgments:

You are very special to us, If you have read this book up to this point or any part of it for that matter. A shoutout to you all for your support. No one, including myself, believed this random thought could ever become a reality. This type of book will never come to fruition without my burgundy rose, Yannie. The ideas and observation within this book is a tribute to all the places (The Caribbean, NY, NJ, OH and MD) that I lived in and to the wonderful women and men that I met along the way. Special thanks to all of them, with their kaleidoscopic personalities and beauties, for putting up with my boring conversations, unprovoked brainstorming sessions on them and for being intermittent targets of "Mes yeux revolver." Also, a special thank you to these X persons with whom I have literally countless conversations about absolutely anything human from within this Time and Space: body, mind, soul, etc.! Thus, literally and figuratively, a piece of all of these amazing folks are sprinkled all over this book through its characters. Go figure!

About The Author:

Nicson Lebrun is a writer in human relatioships and a self-made field researcher in how matrimony alters men's and women's behavior. He lives in the D.C., MD and VA Metro Area.

Table of Contents

Dedications:	2
Acknowledgments:	3
About The Author:	4
Preface	7
Chapter 1 Human Disturbance Ahead!	12
Chapter 2 The Rain Bands	16
Chapter 3 Being on its Path	26
Chapter 4 The Feminine Disturbance	33
Chapter 5 The Access Band	40
Chapter 6 Go! Nuke the Eyewall!	44
Chapter 7 Finding A Pearl in Irminger Sea!	62
Chapter 8 The Masculine Disturbance	90
Chapter 9 The Official Announcement of the Storm	93
Chapter 10 Their Jumping in the Storm!	95
Chapter 11 To The Calm Eye Of The Storm!	97
Chapter 12 Where The Sahel And Sahara Dust Meet the Tropical Clouds	100
Chapter 13 When "Harry" failed to meet "Sally"	108
Chapter 14 Enjoying The Calm Eye Of The Storm	111
Chapter 15 Human Made Disturbance	123
Chapter 16 The Long Way To The Storm	129
Chapter 17 When the North Atlantic Ocean Reconnects with the Caribbean Sea	135
Chapter 18 The Heart's Reasons	139
Chapter 19 Interpreting The Warnings	145
Chapter 20 Securing a "Husband for the Lord!"	153
Chapter 21 The Storm Made By Immigration	159
Chapter 22 To Hunker Down In "The Cushions of The Sea"	166
Chapter 23 A Man's Dilemma	169

Chapter 24 Selecting a Marriage Partner　　　　　175
Chapter 25 How To Anchor Your Man　　　　　　179

Preface

Throughout an individual's life, human love continues to be a crucial and enduring need. All things not being equal, people got married supposedly to secure an ample supply of it, regardless of what had happened to their lives prior. This love is the basis on which lasting and productive relationships are built. It is in this context where the family arrangement has always played an irreplaceable role since the beginning of human history. Within it, young men and women get all encompassing training and support they need to later become themselves well-adjusted adults in the society. In due time, many are expected to form their own family where this healthy cycle will continue for their self-fulfillment and the benefits of the community as a whole.

The family, as an institution, has existed for as long as human civilization itself, making it one of the oldest and most fundamental structures in human society. Its significance cannot be overstated, as the family plays a pivotal role in shaping the development and well-being of individuals and communities alike. Throughout history, strong and cohesive families have been a cornerstone of robust and prosperous societies.

The family unit serves as the primary environment where children are raised and nurtured. When there are children involved, it is within the family that they learn essential values, such as love, compassion, respect, and responsibility. Parents and other family members provide children with guidance, support, and a sense of belonging, which are vital for their emotional, cognitive, and social development. Studies have consistently shown that children who grow up in stable and supportive families are more likely to achieve academic success, develop healthy relationships, and become well-adjusted adults.

Moreover, the family plays a crucial role in preserving and transmitting cultural and spiritual values from one generation to another. Within the family, children are exposed to their culture's language, customs, and beliefs, which shape their identity and sense of belonging to a community. The family also serves as a safety net for its members, providing emotional, financial, and practical support during times of need.

However, such healthy, loving family environments and positive outcomes do not randomly happen. Real work and commitment are required from both partners. Unfortunately, the family as an institution has been under tremendous pressures lately. As a result, it's becoming more and more difficult for couples to remain committed to each other and remain happily married even under the best circumstances. Why? In recent decades, the traditional family structure has undergone significant pressures due to various factors such as prioritization of careers over family, especially by many men, increased female labor force participation, and changing cultural norms. Some people believe that these shifts have resulted in major family problems, including divorces, separations, causing untold trauma for all, especially for the children involved. What are some other pervasive effects of such failures?

The implosion of the institution of marriage has another domino effect on society. For example, they are a growing number of single-parents striving to raise their children without the promised support of long gone partners. Moreover, many cohabiting couples wonder why bother with formal engagement only to become part of this sad, new matrimonial trend. They reasoned that they might be better off with "trial marriages" before committing themselves to traditional, formal relationships. Finally, others decided to spend a lot of resources planning their future divorce, even before they tied the knot with an elaborate prenups agreement! While these alternative family structures can provide love and support to children, they may also face unique challenges and societal stigmas.

If you're married, does it mean that your family is destined to fail? Should the aforementioned discourage you from pursuing marriage if you find a suitable partner? Why investing time and effort in your family is one of the most worthwhile endeavors? These are legitimate questions and concerns. For one needs to be an expert in the field to observe the disturbing trend: that, with each passing decade, more and more marriages seem to fail and tend to last less than during the precedent one. "Why?" many wonder.

Many matrimonial relationships bring real joy, peace and stability within the family circle. Other families, despite experiencing common tribulations, arrive to manage them to live up to their marriage vows. But many others fail to attain such successful outcomes. Some marriage partners, overwhelmed by a rainbow of problems, fail to live up to their initial vows, and walk away when they are needed the most. Still others decide to enter into matrimony with the same mindset of a shopper who goes to his/her favorite store to buy a dress shirt or a formal skirt. Sure! They love the new outfit! It's love at first try! And no wonder! With the store's background music, its lighting or some random compliments from fellow shoppers in the fitting's room vicinity, it's definitely "the one." They may even already envision a special occasion where they would wear it as surely as they would "return" it after the first sensation of discomfort or as soon as they change their mind on the matter. And some have repeated such a disturbing cycle twice or more in a single lifetime! How can someone avoid such soul-stabbing? How to avoid causing so much pain and suffering to their loved ones?

This book, The Human Storm!, delves into the complexities of human relationships, particularly focusing on the dynamics between men and women, from their day to day interaction, mate selection, courtship and into the family setting. Fist of all, like a GPS device, it aims to equip each reader with the ability to do a proper self-appraisal by asking such questions even before entering in a serious relationship or throwing away a current relationship, if he/she is in one right now:

"Why am I the way I am?"

"What kind of childhood did I have?"

"What had happened in my life up to this point?"

"How do my cultural and my formal training background affect me as a person?"

"Today, what kind of person am I as a result of all the above?"

"How have they affected my behavior with my partner and/or my family?"

"As regards to my personality, what are its strengths and weaknesses?"

"Finally, are there some related pitfalls that could lead to self-sabotage or and/or could be toxic to my loved ones? Are some corrective measures needed right now?"

With this kind of updated, objective view of self, a person would be in a better place to have a positive outlook on life. If such deliberate analysis reveals the need for any adjustment (s), there is practical wisdom to either do it BEFORE or being mindful in selecting a partner who would be empathetic and helpful, not potentially sidetracked by it. For "No person should be married to just feel happy. Rather, one should do so to *remain* happy. Second of all, this book proposes a better approach to both assess a person's matrimonial worthiness and an active methodology to select a suitable marriage partner. It reminds its readers that these effective pathways work best once people determine first what the kind of lifestyle they want to have, post their marriage festivities. Then, like a good GPS device, it provides its readers with an analytical perspective on the conflicting forces that will surely come into play within any marital relationships, common challenges, and random pitfalls. It offers step by step guidance on not only how to avoid or maneuver through them but also how to enjoy their mates all along the journey.

What about those who think that they are in a "bad" or "loveless marriage?" We aim to help such couples to stop, think, assess BEFORE giving everything up. This book also helps such readers to understand that in many cases it's not what some people have that's necessarily the main problem. It's rather their attitude and what they do with it that is the culprit! Most folks wouldn't junk their car or bulldoze their place just because something stops working in it. Likewise, we aim to help to develop the same attitude toward their family. Yes, for them to "work with what they have" and how to get the best out of it.

Behind any marriage failure there seems to be a fundamental failure of logic. For example, what a wife may ever want is what her man may lack or isn't presently. As for a typical husband, what he ever wants is maybe to remain a prolific "sower." Naturally, such environments breed male frustration and female suspicion. For such twisted attitudes are eroding the very fabric of healthy and lasting matrimonial relationships. No wonder that "dogs have four legs but can't ever run on so many roads!" Fortunately, though, couples and prospective ones can *choose* the path of commitment and faithfulness. And this book provides them with both the resources and the impetus to do so.

This book is a journey, companion, and guide for self-transformation and empowerment. It addresses your most challenging relationship questions, helping you to contextualize your experiences, your partners' and giving you the tools you'll need on your journey toward both a new outlook that will move you to vouch for your family and toward the creation of the kind of relationship that you so desire.

Chapter 1
Human Disturbance Ahead!

Marriage is a captivating whirlwind that has swept through human history. It is a more potent force than even the fiercest category-five hurricane! However, in countless well-maintained neighborhoods, people gather to glimpse couples standing at the horizon, center stage. It's astonishing how frequently such events unfold in the United States alone, occurring at a breathtaking pace every day. Thousands of couples daringly leap off cliffs, cheered on by family members, friends, and curious onlookers as they ascend the bluffs and descend from the edge. However, despite the jubilant cheers from the crowd, their voices often were pale compared to the intense excitement radiating from the brave individuals taking the plunge.

At the outset of their descent, their enthusiasm is at its peak. The chorus of cheers and the overconfident hope of a brighter future await them below to create an electrifying atmosphere. As time goes on, though, something significant occurs. What could it be? It becomes apparent that the tone of the jumpers' voices undergoes a peculiar transformation. Their emotions seem to navigate the entire spectrum, shifting from euphoria to disappointment, boredom, awkwardness, confusion, fear, and eventually, anger and resentment. For some, external factors like the birth of a child or professional achievements jumble the distinction between these changing dynamics. But inevitably, there comes a point where silence prevails, drowning out the excitement. Unfortunately, "Inverted Gradualism" takes hold at this juncture, and the elusive dream of marital bliss shatters into pieces.

"Why?"

This is the question that millions of individuals around the world continually think and ask, both silently and aloud, when observing this disconcerting reality. After all, they are intelligent people.

Have you ever found yourself wondering about this as well? Perhaps you have, maybe one too many times. What answers have you discovered within yourself or shared with others? We invite you to share your thoughts candidly here, as discussing this significant matter could help you understand that a wall remains a wall, regardless of whether you wish it were a door leading to a more pleasant place. Moreover, your insights could assist countless others in clarifying their thoughts and carefully considering their options before embarking on the quest for marital happiness beneath the sun.

Is a lasting and fulfilling marriage, a "gámos," truly attainable? If so, does it ultimately lead those who seek it to a lifetime of happiness? To start, let's clarify what we mean by "gámos." Suppose you're envisioning the idealized portrayals often seen in Hollywood or the dreams of a future couple and their associates. In that case, you may be in a situation unlike the intrepid "future couples" mentioned earlier. We contend that the conventional concept of marriage is merely an attractive mirage. For it often resembles an arduous journey with an uncertain destination. Do you share this view?

This "book" aims to take you on a journey of self-discovery, where you may encounter something beyond the emotionally scarred bodies or remnants of what love and happiness once looked like at the bottom of the marital peak for so many. We plead with you to navigate through this information with an open mind throughout this journey. If you like what is being shared, use it at your own discretion. If you don't, you can still juggle the information in your head and see how it might benefit you. However, we assure you that nothing untoward will befall you.

The eyewall: Res ipsa loquitur!

In the 21st century, when people encounter a five-and-a-half-month pregnant woman, they would hardly think that it might be a case of a virgin pregnancy! The visible evidence of her swelling belly is reasonably pointing in another obvious direction, Isn't it? Such a neutral observation doesn't imply any involvement in her situation or judgment of it. Instead, it's just an acknowledgment of the reality she faces, neither contributing to her joyride nor her current discomfort and impending pains. Let's refrain from passing judgment, at least for now, and focus on being sensitive to her journey.

Moving forward, let's take a closer look at the complexities of marriage. In the world of relationships, appearances can be deceiving, and what we think we know may not tell the whole story. Therefore, *"res ipsa loquitur"* should guide us as we navigate this challenging terrain. We must endeavor to understand what the facts on the marital ground are trying to convey.

After a storm, we often discover which homes are actually sturdy, regardless of their initial appearances or market values. We realize how fragile they indeed are when countless structures are torn apart. Those who relied solely on geographic coordinates and market values are left regretting their choices. Similarly, the family structure has faced unprecedented pressures since the 1960s, with many families succumbing to countless catastrophic problems. So, what are some of these challenges?

Imagine the happiness and excitement of a newlywed couple, especially during the festive celebrations. It's a perfectly normal feeling. The beginning of any marriage is often filled with joy and hope. Unfortunately, it's common for deadly troubles to emerge on the first night in a "matrimonial paradise." These issues usually have deep

rooted causes that existed long before the couple took their vows.

In some cases, the results can be tragic, as exemplified by the story of Rogerio Damascena, who went from blissful groom to committing a horrifying crime on his wedding night. What could drive a man to such an extreme act? Was it a sudden psychological shock or a realization of betrayal?

Regrettably, it appears that some women also find themselves in unsafe situations in marriage. For instance, a Montana woman was sentenced to 30 years in prison for pushing her husband off a literal cliff in Glacier National Park just eight days after their wedding. It's a stark contrast to their seemingly joyful first dance just days prior. While the horizon may seem idyllic, a closer look reveals a marital landscape that is often fraught with strife, fragility, and monotony. These conditions may be the harsh reality for many in the world of marriage, particularly for those who fail to grasp the complexities of relationships.

If you're considering marriage, tread carefully and ask yourself, "Why?" Entering into matrimony is akin to stepping into quicksand, even with the best intentions and goodwill in the world. Unfortunately, many tentative unions ultimately lead to the drowning of those involved, one way or another. Beneath the surface lie countless spiritually, emotionally, and physically scarred individuals, all casualties of divorce and separation. It's parallel to being blinded by a driver with their high beams on – *distracting and disorienting.*

To find these buried souls, we must overcome the distraction caused by the bright smiles and bridal attire. They are there, and no expertise in family forensics is necessary. Take a moment to reflect on how many members of the family, friends, and acquaintances have become casualties of troubled marriages. It's a sobering reality.

Is it necessary for things to remain this way? If our minds were not constrained, we might pause to contemplate: Why do we witness so many instances of family violence, separations, and divorces, or even the illusion of harmonious families? All the while, everyone seeks to attain the elusive goal of "happiness." It's genuinely confusing that each year in the United States, there are roughly 2.5 million weddings. However, simultaneously, every 13 seconds, a divorce takes place in America. This translates to 277 divorces every hour, 6,646 divorces each day, 46,523 divorces every week, and a staggering 2,419,196 divorces annually – Nevada being the highest in the country. Is this an acceptable reality?

Are you currently in a 'marriage'? If not, do you aspire to be married? Do you ever find yourself feeling hopeless when "Mr. or Mrs. Right" remains elusive? Were you aware that nearly 50 percent of all marriages in the United States will ultimately culminate in separation or divorce? In fact, researchers estimate that 41 percent of all first marriages end in divorce. Would you willingly contribute to these disheartening statistics? If not, perhaps there are some key insights about yourself and your prospective or current partner that you should consider. Could gaining this knowledge lead to a level of satisfaction or even the elusive happiness we all seek?

With this in mind, we aim to share some observations and reflections on the nature of women and men that may shed light on the enigmatic world of family life. Nevertheless, we are mindful of the ancient proverb that wisely states: "The first to state his case seems right until the other party comes and cross-examines him." Thus, your future cross examination is not only expected but warranted!

Chapter 2
The Rain Bands

The Mysterious Half ...

There is an old proverb that says, "It is a snare for a man or a woman to cry out rashly, 'Holy!' And only later to give consideration to what he or she vowed." It seems that too many individuals fall into this trap on the very first day of their married life. No wonder many find themselves trying to understand what's wrong with them and their marriage partners or seeking to untangle themselves during any moments of clarity, whether during the festivities or later. But what makes the institution of marriage such an enticing yet puzzling effort?

Defining Marriage

"A person without knowledge is not good, and the one who acts rashly is sinning," says an ancient maxim. So, what is marriage? We need to go beyond the standard definition and seek a practical, working understanding. Marriage, or Gámos, can be seen as a mutual promise for a future unity. Both partners promise to tame the uncertain future and a sometimes deceptive reality, all within the confines of a complex marital world. However, many newlyweds are unaware of this phenomenon and suffer from what we could call Marriage Lag Disorder or MLD. For some, it's a temporary uneasiness that can be eased with conscientious efforts to adapt to the new marital environment. Unfortunately, for too many, the initial shock is so deep that they never fully recover. They remain legally and religiously married on paper, much like owning a salvaged car after an accident, awaiting the bureaucratic process before letting the once cherished "baby" go to the junkyard. The question is whether MLD is preventable and, if yes, is it treatable? To answer this, we must explore its root causes.

Understanding the nature of human relationship

In a post-Edenic world, defining a man or woman is a vexing challenge. Can we truly capture the essence of humankind today? For example, the Hebrew term for women, 'ish·shah', which can also be translated as "wife," may no longer encompass the fullness of the female phenomenon in the modern world. There seems to be no universal definition of womanhood that can easily encapsulate its essence. For instance, when Well and Good magazine asked 13 women of varying ages and backgrounds the same question, their answers left the readers as reassured as a camel in a sandstorm, thus leaving us disoriented and perplexed.

As a temporary placeholder, we could say that "a woman is a female human being who boldly aspires to become something undefined or to experience certain feelings in the future" (Women = Emotions + Appearance + sexuality + Intellect + X). In the quest for understanding, all we seek is a working definition that can help individuals navigate their identities and relationships. However, it's essential to acknowledge that even the women themselves might not clearly understand their own identity. The notion that women lack self-awareness leads to the assumption that they're uncertain about their desires. This invokes Freud's age-old query, "What do women want?" This enigma has stirred curiosity and debate for decades. Yet, reducing women's complexity to a single question oversimplifies their multifaceted nature. Understanding women's desires requires acknowledging their individuality and diverse experiences. Rather than a universal answer, it's about respecting their autonomy and recognizing the richness of their aspirations.

The Manhood Band

Over the decades since the 1960s, women's growing independence has reshaped their view of men. With increased freedom, their perceptions have shifted, reflecting changing dynamics in relationships and society. This evolution marks a significant journey toward equality and understanding between genders. They no longer see them solely as providers or baby-makers. Instead, they seek partners who can consistently bring positivity, joy, and financial stability into their lives. Many women nowadays view husbands or men as a service, and the most desired ones are those that can be "programmed" to meet their needs. If these husbands could respond to their feminine voice and presence, they would find themselves in higher demand. In such a one-sided family dynamic, the question arises: how long can a typical man remain content in this role?

The disparity between the expectations and perspectives of men and women within marriage often disrupts the equilibrium of the give-and take dynamic. A man entering into marriage typically hopes for his wife to be both "literally and figuratively mild," a concept we'll delve into later. However, many women tend to treat their husbands like voice-activated, two-legged, coin-operated robots at their beck and call, catering to their various desires. Without open and timely communication, frustrations fester, and mutual adjustments fail to materialize. In the absence of corrective measures, the marital arrangement deteriorates, providing no more sustenance than bitter water instead of the promised elephant milk. The couple may still coexist under the same roof, but gradually, they drift apart; they no longer segment the same marital journey or move forward with shared intent, consciously or otherwise. Why does the fiery passion of love often cool so swiftly after the honeymoon phase?

The Romantic Band

The question of romance is undeniably bewildering. It remains an elusive concept that is as vast as the universe itself, touching every corner of humanity in some way or another. In approaching this profound question, we can draw inspiration from the wise words of Desmond Tutu, who once said, "There is only one way to eat an elephant: one bite at a time." Indeed, the question "What is the way of love?" is parallel to that colossal elephant in the world. Unfortunately, no earthly or extraterrestrial definition can fully encompass this complex and multifaceted issue.

Therefore, it becomes our responsibility to make a deliberate effort to gain, at the very least, a working understanding of its true nature to interact with the women and the men in our lives more effectively. This knowledge can prevent us from becoming overwhelmed by their actions and, perhaps most importantly, avoid unintentionally pushing them away. Just as a laborer's hunger drives them to work diligently, so should we approach this monumental question with conscientiousness, taking measured steps towards understanding.

So, let us embark on the journey to address this question with the same mindset and approach. We will begin by examining the following components that contribute to the human-centric equation: Emotions, appearance, sexuality, intellect, background, and the enigmatic "X" factor, all of which collectively contribute to the essence of a man or a woman.

Tropical Waves

"Ah! Our emotions!

Our feelings!

Oh! What a mood they could put us in!

But what would life be without them?

But boy... How they could twist our lives!" (Anonymous)

"If someone responds with "I do" to the second most important question without being aware of the facts, it can lead to foolish and humiliating consequences for both parties involved. Therefore, it is crucial to consider certain key aspects about oneself and one's partner before making such a commitment.

First and foremost, a potential marriage mate should be aware if his future partner has been previously married and may still be connected to her former spouses. This previous marriage might not have been only with men or women, which is a significant detail to consider. It's natural to wonder who or what these previous spouses might be.

Additionally, a meticulous man or woman should take the time to understand his future partner's beliefs and expectations, especially concerning her "deities," before entering into the significant "initiation" ceremony and festivities of marriage. This might involve discussions about religious conversion and the potential implications of a divided household. It's essential to establish clear boundaries and communication regarding these matters.

Another essential aspect to consider is whether one can make their future spouse aware of these facts and the possibility of pursuing a strategic separation from previous partners if necessary. The willingness to accommodate unusual or nonsensical demands without prior notice can also be a vexing challenge for a husband and could lead to challenging reactions from the wife.

Given these considerations, one should ask themselves if, in light of these potential complications, they would still confidently say or have said, "I do."

People are often said to have many "gods," with their emotions being among the most powerful. Emotions can be compared to waves that cannot be prevented, but individuals can choose which ones to navigate. Unfortunately, men and women are swept away or controlled by their emotions, as the following examples illustrate:

1) A king's personal advisor, frustrated by his advice being ignored, left the capital city and took his own life.
2) An older brother, driven by jealousy, killed his younger brother because of the latter's better reputation.
3) A nurse and doctor, on their wedding day, had a tragic end when the husband shot his bride and himself due to a dispute over money.
4) A stepfather's discovery of his wife's online activity led to a fatal argument, highlighting the potential dangers of poorly managed emotions and feelings.

Emotions, feelings, and moods wield immense power, analogous to a tantalizing cocktail that can either enhance our lives or bring about chaos. Much like a double-edged sword, they offer inner protection from life's trials and personal setbacks, but when left unchecked, they can wreak havoc on our minds, bodies, and families, as the cases mentioned above have illustrated. In this exploration, we'll probe into the ingredients that constitute the soul's complicated concoction and their provocative influence on families in their daily lives.

What precisely are the potent tremors of the soul? Emotions are chemical responses triggered by specific stimuli. They create a feedback loop between body and mind, typically lasting for approximately six seconds. On the other hand, feelings manifest as both physical and mental sensations when we internalize these emotions, serving as windows to our innermost selves. Mood, meanwhile, is a composite of emotions and feelings influenced by our surroundings and physical and mental states. When understood, managed, and held in check, these components can indeed enrich our existence, but when allowed to dominate, they can become tyrannical masters. So, let's briefly explore them from both a woman's and a man's perspective before examining how they can wreak havoc on a family when one or both partners succumb to their influence.

Emotions and feelings are the spices of life, akin to seasoning in a dish. When used judiciously, they enhance our experiences and engage all our senses. However, an excess of emotions and feelings in a single dish renders even the finest and healthiest ingredients meaningless. Regrettably, emotions and feelings often hold disproportionate significance in a woman's life. Women tend to identify themselves with their emotions, viewing them as an integral part of their being. The issue lies in the ephemeral nature of feelings; they come and go. Some

individuals may become overwhelmed by their emotions, even allowing them to define their existence. Emotions and feelings hold an almost mystic-like influence over them, serving as guides and lenses through which they perceive themselves, their husbands, and the world around them. What could be the consequences of such perspectives? Can they ever truly find satisfaction in this perpetual state?

Under the right conditions, a twister gains momentum and strength, necessitating careful navigation. The same principle applies to a woman engulfed in her feelings; she becomes both vulnerable and potentially dangerous. The crucial question remains: will her emotions temporarily seize control of her soul, or will she maintain restraint, recognizing that she is distinct from her emotions? The entire family becomes ensnared in this semi-permanent state, influenced by the duchess' reactions to stimuli, whether real or fabricated.

Some people are deeply connected to their emotions, much like sea barnacles clinging to rocks. Their real challenge is distinguishing their feelings from their core selves, which often leads to semi-toxic relationships that can even drive away someone as patient as Romero. It's essential to interpret the following proverbs in this context:

1) "Better to dwell in a corner of the roof than in the same house with a quarrelsome [marriage mate]."
2) "A quarrelsome [marriage mate] is like a constantly leaking roof on a rainy day."
3) "Better to dwell in the wilderness than with a quarrelsome and irritable [marriage mate]."
4) The question arises: how and why does even the sweetest betrothed partner become a source of distress for the soul? Or a menace to the family?

The analogy of the ocean may offer some insight. Waves form due to a combination of factors like water's motion, undercurrents, gravitational forces, and winds. Similarly, in today's fast-paced life, women often grapple with the stress and anxieties arising from their subtle and conflicting aspirations. Additionally, the magnetic pull of femininity generates profound, conflicting inner tremors that can unsettle even the most composed individuals, prompting them to seek refuge in solitude to preserve their sanity.

Consider the aphorism, "If one does not know to which port one is sailing, no wind is favorable." Isn't this principle emblematic of a person who has settled down? Now, envision the state of a wife when she faces not only real challenges but also imaginary ones and external pressures. For her husband, it becomes a bewildering choice between 'fighting' or 'fleeing.' Being with a woman is like drinking 10 cups of coffee on a rotating mechanical bull and reciting verses from your holy book, and still not being confident if you want to continue or get off. In many cases, there is no clear-cut answer; this is the paradox of marriage, my friend.

If one cannot navigate their own emotions, they are akin to unstrapped hay on the Irish coast, vulnerable to external influences. Consequently, this can lead to unforeseen consequences, where misguided individuals may assume authoritative roles and exploit

others. When wives perceive themselves as victims and adopt this identity, they become gossip mongers of ineffective solutions, acting as self-appointed family advisors, the harshest critics of marital issues, and even imposing arbitrary dues systems, resembling the inflexible Vashti or demanding union chiefs with little genuine value to offer. Should husbands invest in any of these offerings, even at a discounted price? Beware of the pitfalls!

Consider the story of a queen who, upon learning of her son's execution, adorned herself with black eye shadow and meticulous attire before meeting the person responsible for her son's death. In that poignant moment, she aspired to present herself at her best. This underscores women's enduring, age-old pursuit to resemble goddesses, driven by the allure of the original promise first mentioned in Genesis. They are willing to take great risks to achieve this coveted divine-like appearance and status, to be irresistibly desired and sought after. However, a question lingers: is there a more certain path to attain this goal than through physical beauty? It seems to be a fundamental credo in the female psyche. The pursuit of this original aspiration appears to be inching closer to reality, thanks to modern-day makeup, scientific advancements, and technology. Yet, one cannot overlook the persuasive efforts of cunning marketers who strive to sell these ideals. In a way, they have become the modern-day equivalent of the original reptilian Tempter, haven't they?

"Beauty has no price," or so goes the enduring credo ingrained in girls from the very moment they inhabit their mother's womb. This proverb, deeply rooted in feminine culture, underscores the significance of beauty in a woman's life. Paying close attention to the wisdom imparted by experts can provide valuable insights into this enigmatic aspect of womanhood. The following anecdote serves as a poignant illustration of this phenomenon.

We happened to overhear a conversation involving Debbie, a close friend of Cattie, who had been grappling with the baffling changes in her younger friend's behavior lately. To label it as "wrong" might be too strong a term, given the amicable nature of their friendship. Nevertheless, Cattie's recent "peculiar" conduct had left Debbie bewildered. It became increasingly evident that whenever Cattie visited Debbie's home, she promptly made a beeline for the restroom, sometimes even before exchanging the customary pleasantries of "Hello" and "How are you?"

Cattie, understandably, exhibited a hint of nervousness when confronted with Debbie's untimely queries, especially considering the proximity of others within earshot. However, the dye had been cast, as elderly individuals often feel entitled to express their thoughts unreservedly. In the interest of sincerity, it was discovered that Cattie had been incorporating a strong laxative tea into her dieting regimen with the sole purpose of inducing frequent bowel movements. This unorthodox practice was her means of shedding pounds in a quest to regain her former svelte self.

It then dawned on us why Cattie had been toting an eight-ounce personal, portable smoothie blender wherever she went during the winter season. In the absence of those dietary indulgences, she resorted to strict adherence to her routine, determined to bid farewell to her stubborn curves. When the inevitable question of "why" finally arose, her explanation did not disappoint any of us. She disclosed that she was preparing for a religious convention scheduled for the next month, and her appearance was of paramount importance. Cattie possessed a dress that she needed to fit into.

Cattie's ultimate goal was to use her appearance as a tool to elicit specific reactions and feelings from those who beheld her. Her commitment to reverting to her pre-pandemic physique reflected a level of determination that could rival even the most Machiavellian strategist.

The pursuit of beauty and the perception thereof occupies a central place in a woman's daily life. Yet, this pursuit is never solely about external appearances. Why, you ask? Because women also yearn to 'feel' desired and beautiful. Above all else, women seek to nurture and sustain the Feminine Beauty's Feedback Loop (FBL), often at great personal expense. But what exactly is the FBL? It summarizes a woman's incessant longing to receive positive feedback regarding her captivating feminine attributes and qualities, whether genuine or otherwise. Many men fall into something similar, the Masculine Ego's Feedbak Loop (MEFL). These cycles are among the most potent influencers shaping a man's and a woman's identity respectively.

Men must acknowledge that some men and women are willing to make significant sacrifices to ensure the uninterrupted continuity of this precious cycle. The FBL and MEFL functions as an invisible force that permeates every facet of a person's life, guiding her choices and actions in its pursuit. However, As seen above, these tremors of the soul are indeed ambivalent masters that naturally run on both human lanes!

Contrary to popular belief, men experience the full spectrum of human emotions. So they move them just like they influence everybody else, but education, culture, religion and other social factors tend to inhibit how men live through and manifest their feelings. So it's a misconception to believe otherwise. For example, society often tells men to be stoic and avoid showing emotions like sadness or vulnerability. This tends to lead men to unhealthy skin bottling up their feelings or sometimes expressing them in less healthy ways, like violent outbursts.

Men often weren't taught how to express their malaise even within their family circle. Later, such inability could create unnecessary tension in their relationships. In other cases, they may have trouble putting words on their emotions or struggle to share them with others. Potentially it can also lead to frustration and make it a chore to deal with family members and friends, even with their partners. As a result, they might turn to destructive coping mechanisms like a sudden or gradual withdrawal from loved ones, substance abuse, or risky behavior.

Chapter 3
Being on its Path

Emmie's story revolves around a young woman who endured the tragic loss of both her parents during her childhood. Lacking any affluent relatives willing to support her after becoming an orphan, Emmie found herself stuck in poverty throughout her adult life. She despised her impoverished circumstances, often telling herself, "I must discard it like unwanted trash."

However, Emmie received life-changing advice from an older woman one day. She learned that despite facing poverty, she didn't have to show it outwardly. Realizing her neglected self-care hid her natural beauty, she likened herself to the Mona Lisa veiled under a shroud. Determined, she followed the woman's guidance, dressing neatly and improving her self-care. Within months, her transformation was remarkable, almost like a whole new person emerged.

During this transformative period, Emmie crossed paths with a man in his late forties who was drawn to her not only for her physical attributes but also for her inner qualities. He offered her marriage, and she eagerly accepted, recognizing it as the quickest route out of her poverty-stricken life. With a husband now and being in her late twenties, Emmie had seemingly left her past far behind, but the question remained: could she maintain this newfound stability in her life?

The essence of a successful marriage elicits pondering. What does a person truly desire in a marriage, and how can one keep their partner engaged and content? Jim, Emmie's husband, not only provided for her basic needs but also cherished and protected her, as any imperfect man would. Her life had become comfortable and respectable. At this point, she appeared to have numerous reasons for happiness, even enjoying the company of her new friends. However, Jim's intuition raised concerns about the sustainability of their relationship despite no reasonable basis for his unease at that time. Preferring to prevent issues rather than solve them later, Jim reasoned that a change in geography might be beneficial. So, he decided to relocate to an exclusive and reputable neighborhood with his young new wife, hoping that respectability and privilege would deter temptations.

Jim's uneasiness paralleled the concerns of the Shulammite brothers, who constantly worried about the onslaught of male attention and allurements their young and beautiful sister would have to resist to maintain her moral integrity as she matured. They wondered if her days of innocence were numbered:

"We have a little sister, and she has no breasts.

What would we do for her…?

On the day when she is spoken for or

when daylight shines forth on her fetching beauty?

If she is a wall,

We will build upon her a battlement of silver,

But if she is a door,

We will board her up with a cedar plank."

So, would Jim's Emmie be like a wall or a lockless garden gate? Would an apparently "good and secure" neighborhood offer her enough protection against the allure of stolen waters? Only time will tell.

One day, Emmie went for a solo walk in a nearby city park at twilight with Sylk, her new puppy. The park was dog-friendly, attracting a diverse group of people who came regularly at that time to enjoy the variety of flora and the multitude of souls. There, she encountered DuBoyd, an elegant and eloquent young man who owned a downtown apartment in a chic neighborhood. As usual, it all started with the man's best friend.

"What a cutie! What breed is it?" inquired the curious young man.

"A Maltese," answered Emmie.

"How old is he?" he continued.

"Almost two years. We got *her* when she was just one year old. It feels like we got her just yesterday!" she said with a smile.

"Absolutely! Those tiny bundles of joy can really keep us on our toes. Their endless love and unstoppable energy make each day an adventure. It's like they have this special power to banish boredom and loneliness, especially in today's world. We're truly fortunate to have them around," the young man remarked, drawing Emmie into contemplation with his words.

"True, but at times, I feel like the speed of time is a threat to my "*Forever 21*" motto. I really hate the idea of growing old and frail!" she quickly added.

"Allow me to introduce myself, I'm DuBoyd. Aging hasn't been my favorite topic either, but seeing you erases any worry. You're like the vast, timeless horizon, radiating beauty that echoes through the ages, reminiscent of the biblical Sarah!" DuBoyd admitted, finding solace in the timeless allure mirrored in the person before him.

Emmie's cheeks flushed with embarrassment as she replied, "Oh, DuBoyd! Thank you so much. But I'm certain you must encounter countless girls who are far more stunning and refined than I am, particularly in a flirty city like this. Tell me I'm not lying! Am I?"

"To the contrary, I have a confession to make," the young man replied.

Emmie, now curious and anxious, asked, "Really? A confession? What for?"

He paused for what felt like an eternity before saying the following heart-flattering words, "All my life, my dream was always to one day meet the most beautiful woman in the world. Fortunately, at this moment in time, I no longer have such a desire."

"Why? What happened?" she wondered anxiously.

"Because looking at you today convinced me that she could never be more beautiful than you are," continued DuBoyd.

With those carefully crafted, perfectly timed words, DuBoyd effectively blew her mind away and momentarily swept her off of her feet, so to speak. Though no cheese fell off the ground at that time, sooner or later, something else was going to give. But keep in mind that what is "nothing" for a woman could be and would be a life-altering catastrophe for her husband, and vice versa. For Emmie, though, now is not the time for such considerations. The worker deserves his wages... However, how do women usually reward those who keep their feedback loop alive?

What might prevent her from straying down the primrose path? It was undeniable that the gentleman's generous compliment had warmed Emmie's heart, and her ego and vanity had been thoroughly indulged. But were there more important things to consider? Perhaps her fresh new marriage or the preservation of her self-respect?

"DuBoyd, thank you... Do you truly believe that?" Emmie asked, her voice tinged with uncertainty. "Am I really that... beautiful…?"

"Stop jesting, DuBoyd. Are you being sincere?" Emmie mumbled, trying to process his flattering words and regain her footing, if that was even possible under such circumstances. Still shaken with flattery, she hastily gave him a cheeky goodbye kiss, a tantalizing glimpse into what the future might hold.

Was it too late for her? DuBoyd seemed to have struck gold! They exchanged contact information, ostensibly to continue their intriguing conversations...

When Emmie returned home that night, she felt like a compromised computer system infiltrated by a skillful black hat hacker. She struggled to maintain a facade of normalcy in Jim's presence, but her soul was wandering aimlessly, preoccupied with a dangerous secret. If only Sylk could talk, Jim would have known the precarious situation they were all in! Indeed, DuBoyd's influence was like a bug, silently spreading, and it was only a matter of time before the damage became visible to all parties involved. She had the urge to call or text him before going to bed that night, but her better judgment then prevailed for obvious reasons. But would reason ever triumph in these typical circumstances?

The following weekend, while Emmie was shopping downtown at the mall, DuBoyd messaged her superficially to inquire about her and Sylk. Jim was working from home that day, taking care of their puppy. Emmie took the bait and decided to call DuBoyd instead of texting, eager to share everything that had transpired since their last encounter in the park. DuBoyd listened patiently and attentively, like a skilled hunter, and it worked like a charm. She felt relieved and comfortable, unburdening her feelings that day. It was as though she had known him for ages.

"Why isn't my husband like DuBoyd?" Emmie wondered. "He's such a genuine and empathetic listener," she mused. "Emmie, you're a sensitive woman, and you have such a lovely and enchanting voice.

I wish it could be the last thing I hear every night before bed," DuBoyd commented, paying close attention to every word she said. It was easy to see why many engaged women could fall into his trap. Would Emmie prove to be one of the few exceptions?

Emmie suddenly felt warmth, not from the weather or any modern indoor comfort system but from the genuine connection she had developed with DuBoyd. However, a text from her husband reminding her to pick up vanilla-flavored whey protein at the mall for him interrupted the moment. But before that interruption, at that moment in time, only geographical distance provided any "sursis" to Jim's marriage, even if it was temporary at best.

Women sometimes prioritize romantic promises over hard facts, especially when their ego is stroked or their desires reinforced. Married partners often grapple with the notion that "A bird in the hand is worth two in the bush." So, early in the fall season, while Jim was busy with yard work on a Friday afternoon, Emmie headed to her usual downtown pet store to buy dog food for her puppy.

As she reached the cashier's terminal and pulled out her card to pay, she noticed Duboyd's address on a contact card he had given her in the park some time ago. Her heart raced, her pulse soaring to over 100 beats per minute at the mere thought... However, her reverie was interrupted when the cashier asked, "What's your zip code, ma'am?"

Sitting in her car, she couldn't resist entering Duboyd's address into her cellphone's GPS. To her surprise, she discovered that Duboyd lived only three blocks away. Curiosity got the best of her, and she hesitantly sent Duboyd a WhatsApp message: "Are U... home...?"

"Yes, unfortunately, alone, winding down watching a baseball game on TV," he replied.

"And U?" he asked.

"Just three blocks away from your place!" she admitted.

"What an opportunity, Emmie! You should come to see where I live! I won't take no for an answer!" Duboyd insisted.

Unable to resist, Emmie found herself at his door. Her heart was racing. There was a conflict between her heart and mind and a war between lust and reason, like a ci-ça struggle being played out at her core. Something was telling her that it was not the right thing to do.

But, the sensations down below in her loin and the adrenaline rush got the best of her. In a bold move, she parked outside in front of his apartment. She came prepared for an illicit encounter, and, under such circumstances, lust got the best of her senses, jeopardizing her family and her own sense of personal dignity. So they vigorously exercised their lust!

Pase lo que pase!

After a partial clean-up in the downstairs bathroom, Emmie quickly fakes a goodbye kiss to the exhausted Duboyd and rushes to get home before Jim notices her extended absence. She almost forgot her panties, which were sitting on the top of the couch in the living room. In a hurry, she put them into her handbag. Still fixing herself as she drove off, Emmie decided it would be wise to create an alibi, just in case. So, she stopped at the coffee shop near her place to put her underwear on in the bathroom and to get her beloved husband his favorite pumpkin drink.

"There were so many customers at the café today, and at the pet store, one would think they were giving away free stuff," she thought, in case Jim asked why it took her so long. "Thanks, sweetie, for the drink. It's like you read my mind," Jim said after she handed it to him. Emmie placed her puppy's food in the fridge and told Jim, "I am going to take a shower upstairs and be down in a minute," as he continued watching TV in the living room after his afternoon work outside the house.

About thirty minutes later, as she descended the stairs, Emmie reassured herself, saying, "I am clean, whole, and here I am! Truly, jabbing the lake left no marks at all." She pretended to be available for her husband, but deep down, she felt physically depleted and had no desire for him. Her attitude mirrored that of women in an old Hebrew proverb: "This is the way of an adulterous woman: She eats, she wipes her mouth; Then she says, 'I have done nothing wrong.'"

Upon seeing Emmie in her negligee as she came down, Jim made room for her with a smile. For him, it would be a lovely afternoon like countless others, but for her, it marked the beginning of the end. Why? Because sooner or later, their young marriage would join the grim statistics of 2,419,196 divorces that occur every year in the US alone. At one point in her life, Emmie longed for comfort, stability, and security. Once Jim provided all of that, all she had ever desired was

Duboyd, precisely what her provider could never be. Like her, many married partners each year find or invent all-too-human reasons to jeopardize the stability they once craved in favor of chasing their own desires.

The statement, "The face of a Woman is a source of corruption" for men not related to them, was made by a prominent religious and political spokesman as an explanation for the requirement that women wear all-enveloping *burqas* when going out, and even then, only when accompanied by a male relative. This perspective aligns with the new purity movement, which suggests that, ultimately, women and girls bear the responsibility for the sexual thoughts, feelings, and choices made by men. According to this view, it is incumbent upon women and girls to dress, act, and speak in a manner that ensures non-sexuality for all people. Failure to do so may result in their being labeled as impure or harlots.

The question that arises is whether women truly possess such an irresistible influence or if this belief instead underscores men's willingness to abdicate their own responsibility in their interactions with the opposite sex.

Chapter 4
The Feminine Disturbance

It's often emphasized in capitalist markets that the consumer holds a position of utmost importance. Who wouldn't want to wield such power and enjoy its accompanying privileges? Eddy experienced a similar dynamic with his first wife, Zonelle, who was youthful, energetic, and animated. They tied the knot at a young age in Queens, NY. Zonelle's attitude was that her 'hard-working' husband was the caretaker of her garden, *Il Giardino*, even though she owned it. To him, she was his beloved, and their life together was a source of delight.

Throughout most weeks, except for roughly 12 of them, Zonelle's presence transformed their home into a fruitful orchard with an abundance of easily accessible "fruits" for Eddy, which brought him immense satisfaction. Each day, before going to sleep or work, she would lovingly say, "Miele, the gate is about to close; now is the time to enjoy the fruits if you wish." This sentence had always held a special allure for him. It goes without saying that in such an environment, there was no room for frustration or chronic headaches; their home was indeed a paradise on Earth. Zonelle also managed to introduce Eddy to a healthy diet rich in feminine delicacies, a tradition he fondly remembered even long after her untimely passing. He missed her deeply, and his two subsequent marriages were a failed attempt to find a new Zonelle.

However, each of these marriages proved challenging in its own way. His subsequent wives tended to focus more on their individual interests and less on the figurative "orchard" they were supposed to nurture together. Eddy's third wife, Samarid, acted more like a business partner than the well-rounded companion she had initially promised to be. Now in his 60s and married to his fourth wife, Eddy continues to search for a suitable replacement for his original "orchard." He wonders if modern society can still produce wives who embody the sweetness he once cherished.

There are a couple of important insights that all individuals, whether married or not, should bear in mind about relationships with women. One such understanding can be gleaned from a space-related analogy. A black hole is an astronomical phenomenon where gravity is so intense that even light cannot escape. Despite its name, a black hole is far from empty space; instead, it consists of an enormous amount of matter compressed into a remarkably small space. Envision a star ten times more massive than the Sun condensed into a sphere approximately the size of New York City.

Although not visible to the naked eye, there is ample scientific evidence of black holes in the cosmos. Now, on Earth, throughout history and even today, some influential individuals have held strong beliefs that women, and particularly their physical attributes, exert a similar irresistible gravitational pull on the men around them. Some have even argued that this pull indirectly contributes to humanity's erratic course. So, the question arises: Is it true that women's physical presence exerts a comparable force on men? If so, what is the nature of this force, and how forceful is it? Unlike the inescapable pull of a black hole's gravity, is the attraction to femininity something that can be resisted or managed? And if so, is there a safe zone or a certain distance that can protect one from being metaphorically "pulled in"?

There appears to be an intriguing and compelling force intrinsic to women when it comes to their allure, a force that wields significant influence. Just as the gravitational pull of a black hole manifests through its impact on nearby objects, the seemingly irresistible attraction of femininity becomes abundantly clear when examining the following accounts of real-life events. The pressing issue was how to counter an invincible army steadily advancing towards the border—a mystery that troubled Balak, a formidable Moabite king, approximately 1500 years before Christ's era. In response, he convened a war council within the confines of his chamber, assembling his military commanders, war strategists, pertinent cabinet members, and trusted advisers to strategize for the impending battle.

With apprehension in his voice, the king probed his top brass, "How soon will the enemy soldiers reach our borders? Are we adequately prepared for effective combat? Can we emerge victorious against the Israelite army as our current circumstances stand?" The response came from one experienced general, "Our estimation places the might of the Israelite forces at over half a million, and they are indeed formidable. Yet, so are our own mighty warriors. While their generals may possess cunning, they lack the battlefield prowess we Canaanites have honed. The Sons of Israel wield swords and spears, as do we, but we possess chariots they do not. Our cities are fortified while they dwell in camps. We are intimately acquainted with the terrain, whereas they are strangers to it. In every military aspect, we hold the advantage. Yet, unlike any we have faced before, they are formidable adversaries, and our people's hearts are filled with apprehension," the generals reported.

After a thorough assessment of all available options, a unanimous decision was reached, even among the most hawkish members of the council. They concurred that employing the subtlest of powers could prove to be the most effective and efficacious weapon against this challenging army. Consequently, in accordance with the king's decree, court officials scoured the kingdom's territory for exceptionally beautiful young women, carefully selecting only those who possessed the qualities of Abishag of old. These chosen ones were then brought to the capital city, where they underwent beauty treatments and received specialized training in what was termed "strategic seduction" tactics.

However, it became evident that they required more young beauties than Moab alone could provide to assemble this extraordinary army. As a result, emissaries from the Moabite King were dispatched to his neighboring ally, the King of Midian, seeking additional participants for this cause. Subsequently, an official convoy of Midianite women arrived in Moab to join their local counterparts, all undergoing state-sponsored preparations for this top-secret mission. The question loomed: Who would gain the upper hand in this battle between flesh and forged steel? The stakes could not have been higher for all parties involved.

Meanwhile, Israel and its army had encamped on the desert plains of ancient Moab. Under the cover of night, a regiment of Moabite and Midianite "special forces" took position, preparing for a surprise assault. Stealthily, numerous squads of Moabite and Midianite Abishags and their Midianite *bambolinas* approached the Israelite camp, poised to employ their feminine "weapons" in service of their respective nations. Their target: courageous, strong, and valiant Israelite career soldiers. In effect, they seduced them. The Moabite and Midianite women enticed many Israelite males into acts of sexual promiscuity and depraved idolatry. The outcome? Those vulnerable Moabite and Midianite Abishags and bambolinas, either directly or indirectly, were implicated in the demise of approximately 24,000

Israelite men, including 1,000 esteemed leaders among them. Who got the power?

King David's anguish was palpable to anyone who observed him; no sharp discernment was necessary to perceive it. His distress was so tangible that even those with the slightest ounce of empathy could feel it. Yet, his torment was most eloquently expressed through his own words:

"[...] My bones were wasted away because of my groaning all day long." "My strength evaporated like water in the dry summer heat."

What could have induced such profound desolation in a king of his stature? What were the underlying reasons? Was it the result of a significant military setback, or did it stem from the sorrow of losing a cherished loved one? Should you grant us the opportunity to narrate his tale, you might come to realize that his story is as common as the changing of seasons.

David possessed a blend of virtues that included courage, fairness, sympathy, and integrity, rendering him a caring and responsible individual throughout his life. However, let us momentarily concentrate on the events leading up to the pivotal "until" to appreciate the remarkable resilience of a woman's strength. Despite being the youngest of eight siblings, his father entrusted him with the crucial role of overseeing the family's flock, a weighty responsibility considering the pivotal role livestock played in sustaining their livelihood in ancient Israel. He displayed unflinching bravery in safeguarding the flock. On a particular day, a lion and a bear threatened the flock, presenting him with a harrowing dilemma: to flee or to confront the challenging adversaries. David opted for the latter and, in the act of remarkable valor, vanquished both the lion and the bear, fearsome beasts that would have wrecked the nerves even of the most intrepid of hearts.

In a later chapter of his life, David encountered another seemingly insurmountable adversary: Goliath, the towering 9 feet 6 inches giant from Gath. A veritable behemoth of a man!

Picture the scene: a young shepherd pitted against a battle-hardened warrior in a pivotal showdown. What led their paths to intersect at that precise moment in time? In brief, David had become a court musician and arm-bearer in the service of Saul, the reigning king, who was embroiled in a fierce conflict with the arch-nemesis of

Israel, the Philistines. Conversely, Goliath was a battle-seasoned champion for his people, likely dedicating his entire adult life to warfare. He brazenly challenged any man from the Israelite ranks to engage in single combat and resolve the war once and for all. This provocation endured for over a month as the entire Israelite army quaked in fear, from the lowest-ranking soldier to the commander-in-chief and every high-ranking official in between. It appeared, in retrospect, as a dire moment similar to the "*Black Hawk Down*" incident for the Israelite forces. But would it indeed culminate in a similar catastrophic retreat? Remarkably, as mentioned earlier, the young David volunteered to face the Philistine giant on his own. He proceeded to defeat Goliath decisively in that extraordinary battle.

Would you have dared to accept such a daunting challenge? David did so fearlessly and courageously, confronting terrifying enemies and emerging victorious on all three occasions.

His triumph over the Philistine giant elevated David to the status of a national hero, dramatically altering the course of his life. Soon after, King Saul entrusted him with leadership over his army, and David achieved widespread acclaim through numerous victories. Regrettably, the king's jealousy of David's military prowess led to a vow to kill him, transforming David into a perceived enemy of the state of Israel. King Saul, along with his intimidating force of 3000 elite soldiers, relentlessly pursued David like a hunted animal for several years. Life as a fugitive was anything but peaceful or agreeable. Despite the ordeal, David remained steadfastly loyal, even to the wicked king, refusing to take his life on multiple occasions, even when it might have meant finally returning home. Throughout these trials, David upheld his moral integrity as a man of God, refraining from seeking vengeance for fear of becoming blood guilty. However, during another military campaign against the Philistine army, King Saul took his own life after sustaining grave injuries in a fierce battle. Finally, after enduring years on the run, David was liberated from this arduous foe without compromising his commitment to righteousness and integrity.

It has often been remarked that there is no harm in indulging one's curiosity by looking. While this assertion may hold some truth, it is essential to acknowledge that the impact of looking can vary widely depending on the context, the individuals involved, and their intentions. Looking at it may not be a problem, but what and why could easily cause serious harm with far-reaching consequences. Let me share a story from the past to illustrate this point.

On a balmy spring day, a gorgeous Israelite woman named Bathsheba was taking an outdoor bath. Unbeknownst to her, King David, her neighbor, happened to be on the rooftop of his palace and laid eyes upon her, describing her as "very good in appearance." What unfolded next was a tale of fatal attraction that would trouble King David's soul for the rest of his life.

Overcome by Bathsheba's sexual appeal, David momentarily forgot about his seven wives and numerous concubines. Moreover, Bath-sheba was already married to another fellow countryman who happened to be a fine soldier in his army. Despite the supposed brevity of their encounter, driven by desire, David brought her into the palace and engaged in a sexual escapade. This affair, considering their marital statuses, could be seen as an infamous one-night stand, perhaps one of the first recorded in biblical history. However, David's infatuation led him to claim exclusive possession of Bathsheba, ultimately orchestrating the demise of her husband. He then added the newly widowed Bathsheba to his harem.

In the grip of his carnal desires, a sexually obsessed David cast aside his noble qualities, such as courage, fairness, sympathy, and integrity—virtues he had once held dear. He willingly sacrificed everything for the sake of countless encounters with Bathsheba. This transformation was so profound that this same David, who had previously spared a wicked king intent on killing him, even in self-defense, now ordered the death of Bathsheba's innocent husband, Uriah the Hittite, simply because he was her lawful spouse.

David's remorse and depression were intense once he regained his senses. Later, he composed poetic words that aptly expressed the darkness of that chapter in his life. It begs the question—could any of us, in good conscience, cast the first stone? The answer is clear—no reasonable individual would dare to do so.

At this juncture, there should be no doubt about the powerful sway a woman's physical presence can hold over a man. We've seen that even heavenly beings, devoid of typical human sexual desires, succumbed to the allure of earthly women. These celestial beings forsook their divine station to descend to Earth, not for meaningful conversations or companionship but for physical intimacy or purely sex. They, too, fell under the spell of the ancient *Bellissimas*.

Thus, it appears that intelligent beings, regardless of their celestial origins or earthly abode, cannot escape the feminine form and its essence's magnetic attraction. This leads us to reflect on the age-old Hebrew proverb:

"[...] A woman's breasts can captivate and intoxicate a man at all times and beyond recovery."

The overarching lesson from this narrative is that men, of their own accord and without coercion, have been willing to relinquish everything for the allure of a woman. Some have abandoned their families, forsaken their religious beliefs, political power, defied their racial and societal identities, and surrendered their fame and social status. Others have gone to extreme lengths, resorting to murder or incest, seemingly unable to resist the gravitational pull of the feminine.

It's crucial to emphasize that a man is rarely swayed or convinced by a woman's words or arguments; instead, he surrenders to his own senses and envisions future opportunities, like a person with a substance abuse disorder drawn to the promise of another indulgent experience. Likewise, for a man, the cost of such pursuits becomes inconsequential in the face of a woman's allure, akin to the relentless pull of an addictive drug. After all, who can ever claim to have had their fill of a woman's irresistible charms?

Chapter 5
The Access Band

"Pay for play" or "marry to play"? After exchanging vows, no husband ever anticipated grappling with such a question because she had privately and publicly pledged him unrestricted and complete access to her heart, mind, and every inch of her body. Those commitments were even documented! This assurance sufficed for any prospective husband, understanding that promises are irrespective of unforeseen circumstances in the unpredictable world. Nevertheless, the wedding rituals typically transform the once dedicated fiancée into a whole new entity—a married woman. Thus, sometime after the honeymoon, she may adopt an attitude akin to the US at the conclusion of the Cold War. Sooner or later, the cards must be reshuffled and dealt with by the new sheriff. This marks a new world order, leaning towards the latter! The days of a free lunch, as promised, are over. And about the weekly buffet that husbands often expect? Absolutely out of the question. In this post-legal phase of the divine institution, randomness gives way to a systematic pay-for-play approach. No longer the give-and-take relationship, such an attitude would usher us into the land of sexuslism, where women utilize their sensuality as a versatile tool.

So, what exactly is sexuslism? It's a self-motivated family dynamic where a woman wields sexual intimacy or her realm of pleasures as both a reward and a punishment. Ultimately, she holds dominion over the market – her husband – both horizontally and vertically. There are no established rules, and it appears there is no antitrust agency to oversee matters either. Men, it's crucial to understand how this market operates. Why, you ask?

Consider this: do you prefer your woman with or without restrictions? Rest assured, we're on the same page here. Unfortunately, she's aware of this as well. So, be cautious about what you desire! The real estate location principle comes into play here. Why? All else being equal, where they metaphorically put their "undies" after wearing them would determine the family's ambiance and longevity.

The following story illustrates sexuslism as a potent double-edged sword. Tarah married Johnny, a computer repair technician. Customers dropped off their machines at his place for repairs and left them there until these machines were ready to be picked up. Over time, a considerable number of broken CPU towers, monitors, and machines accumulated, awaiting repair or pickup. Most wives wouldn't tolerate such a desecration of their home for long, and Tarah was no exception. Day in and day out, she repeatedly asked Johnny, often nagging him, to remove the clutter from her living space. "I'll take care of it tomorrow," he would promise. Yet, for months on end, tomorrow never arrived! Frustrated, Tarah decided to employ her "secret weapon" in order to "compel" him to cooperate. One day, while Johnny was working downstairs, she entered her bedroom and donned her honey birdette lingerie set. At that moment, Tarah was acutely aware of her irresistible allure. She had trained herself in the art of seduction from an early age. Her allure was scorching, her bosom ablaze with intensity and erected like forged swords. Maintaining a strategic distance from him, she informed Johnny that she'd be open to providing some warmth in his chosen area if he would only organize his computer clutter or remove it altogether.

As Johnny saw his wife in all her glory, his heart started racing and pumping blood at the other head. His adrenaline surged instantly, and his heart raced dangerously. Without hesitation, he stood and hastily rearranged his possessions or relocated some of them out of her sight. Everything was now in order for him, at least in his mind. He was prepared. However, unfortunately, not everything he did aligned with her expectations. Johnny was left seething, viewing his wife's actions as an unforgivable transgression. Needless to say, their marriage did not endure the test of time!

In the world of marketing, sex can be a powerful tool for persuasion. Similarly, within the context of marital relationships, sex can often become a means through which women exert influence and assert control. In the framework of capitalism, when demand surges, prices typically follow suit, reflecting the dynamics of supply and demand. Many women understand that limiting access to sex can make someone more compliant. A moglie can gauge whether they hold a dominant position depending on the relationship dynamics. Unfortunately, men's appetite for periodic sex consumption appears endless. Women are adept at using sex and intimacy as leverage or punishment, even against reasonable husbands. The challenge for the latter is knowing when to comply or become as embittered as Johnny. Yet, women must consider if their partners who are accustomed to receiving sex or no-strings-attached "benefits from friends" would stay committed long-term. It's a matter of balancing needs and expectations. At times, women's random use of their carrots to manipulate men could be super deadly. Woe to those who remain in a daze! What follows is a true story.

Franky is a teenager deeply attracted and infatuated with a sweet bambolina from his high school whom we would call Lily. So he kept asking her to go out with him whenever an occasion presented itself if he didn't create it. So all his friends, even Lilly, knew about his feelings for her. Though she enjoys the attention, Lilly doesn't even have a slice of platonic love for the poor young man. But Franky was persistent. He thought that somehow, by wear and tear, he would eventually win her over in due time.

Many months have passed, but Lilly's initial feelings haven't changed a bit in the direction Franky would like them to. Consequently, she even became annoyed or angry that he wouldn't take her firm and serial nos for answers. However, one day after class, against all expectations, Lilly told Francky that she would accept to go out with him that weekend, under only one condition: if he would pin his testicles! On hearing that, Franky became euphoric, riding high on the idea that Lilly's attractive ends would amply justify the mean! Still filled with excitement on his way home, he started to think about what he would need, how and where he would fulfill his part of the bargain.

A few days later, with the house empty with no siblings there, Franky descended into the dimly lit confines of his basement bathroom, tasked with a mission he couldn't ignore. The agony pulsating through him was beyond measure, a relentless force threatening to consume him entirely. Yet, amidst the torment, he clung to a flicker of hope, a belief that somehow, amidst the pain, there lay a glimmer of redemption at the other end of the bargain.

With grim determination, he resolved to fulfill the requested deed. It was his turn to uphold the pact, to demonstrate his loyalty. In return, Lilly had promised to arrange a romantic rendezvous, a fleeting escape from the monotony of their everyday lives.

As the afternoon sun of the following day cast long shadows across the empty corridors of the school, Franky sought out Lilly, eager to claim his reward. But the anticipation quickly turned to disbelief as her words pierced through the air like shards of glass.

"You did what, Franky?" Lilly's incredulous voice echoed off the walls, leaving him stunned. "I was just joking. You're so stupid and pathetic. I could never be interested in someone like you."

With those crushing words, Franky's world crumbled around her. Tears welled up in his eyes as he retreated home, the weight of his shattered dreams bearing down upon him like a crushing burden.

In the days that followed, the pain in Franky's groin only intensified, a relentless reminder of his folly. Eventually, medical intervention became unavoidable, and doctors were forced to remove his perforated testicle, ravaged by infection.

What was the purpose of it all? Was there some inherent flaw in Franky's character that led him down this path? Before casting judgment, pause and consider the complexities of human nature. For in Franky's actions, we see reflections of our own desires and vulnerabilities. Men, driven by the promise of pleasure, often find themselves grappling with the consequences of their choices, willing to endure unimaginable pain in pursuit of fleeting lustful moments of ecstasy. So, before condemning Franky, look within yourself, for in his story lies a mirror of the human condition.

Chapter 6
Go! Nuke the Eyewall!

What do women or men truly desire? To achieve ultimate satisfaction, particularly within the context of marriage? Is it the pursuit of a flawless husband, the joys of motherhood, or perhaps the attainment of an overall perfect life? Could it be the serenity of a harmonious relationship with the Higher Power or the aspiration to attain a divine-like status themselves? Is it the quest for power, financial security, or the simple desire to be deeply cherished by their partner? Indeed, what is this elusive "Thing" that would bring contentment to women? Many men's husbands would willingly offer a significant portion of our resources to ensure their wives' happiness and fulfillment. Yet, despite men's or women's earnest efforts, it often feels like they're navigating through uncharted territories, attempting to translate the complexities of the human psyche. It seems, past the newlywed period, folks tend to fixate on what the other partner isn't or on what it lacks.

It's ingrained in men to strive to provide for the object of their affection, to ensure that their offerings align with their beloved's evolving desires and needs. This perpetual concern stems from the fear of failing to uphold the exclusivity of their relationship, both physically and emotionally. Thus, men have tirelessly pursued various avenues, hoping to capture the essence of beauty and satisfy the depths of their partner's soul. Yet, despite centuries of endeavor, a definitive and enduring strategy remains elusive. Indeed, the quest to understand and fulfill satisfactorily the desires of a marriage partner continues to challenge and intrigue us all.

Ah, the allure of comfort! Who wouldn't crave the snug embrace of contentment? Comfort, that blissful state of both body and mind, is often hailed as liberation from pain, distress, and constraint. Indeed, the desire for comfort resonates deeply with women everywhere, a universal truth that Ted Berstein's story poignantly underscores.

In the narrative of Ted's life, we witness a journey marked by pursuing this delicate balance. Like any devoted partner, Ted had pledged to Brea, his fiancée, that he would diligently strive to furnish her with such comfort in due time. Yet, the reality of their circumstances post-marriage led them to settle for a modest one-bedroom apartment in a less-than-ideal neighborhood—a compromise dictated by financial constraints. The urgency of matrimony momentarily eclipsed the initial discomfort of this reality, a decision made amidst discussions and plans tinged with unease.

Brea's aspirations for material comfort were clear from the outset, a fact that Ted couldn't ignore. Her vision painted a picture of idyllic living—a spacious home in a desirable neighborhood adorned with modern amenities and tasteful furnishings. Such desires, while reasonable, often serve as tangible markers of success for men, yet they find themselves at the mercy of their partners' ever-changing preferences.

The early years of Ted and Brea's union, save perhaps the honeymoon phase, proved to be a trial by fire—a period of adjustment and mutual learning. Their journey through married life, punctuated by moments of disappointment, failure, and unmet expectations, demanded resilience and adaptability. Intimacy, once a frequent occurrence, waned in the face of the demands of everyday life as they poured their energies into securing their livelihood.

Their commitment to each other remained steadfast, albeit tested by the strains of parenthood and the constraints of their modest living space. With the arrival of their daughter Aubrie, joy mingled with the burden of added obligation, particularly for Ted, who found himself directing Brea's fluctuating emotions while shouldering the responsibilities of a demanding job and the care of a newborn in cramped quarters.

The Bersteins' journey has been fraught with challenges, yet their resolve remains unshaken, ever resilient like Lavender flowers. Their determination to provide for their family, no matter the obstacles, is a testament to their resilience and unwavering bond.

After years of persistence, Ted and Brea found themselves inching closer to their American Dream. They both recently graduated from college, with Brea becoming a nurse and Ted earning a degree in database administration. They were now firmly established in their respective fields and ready to take the next step. The promise of purchasing their own home, made by Ted, was finally within reach after a year of hard work. The thought of owning their first house in charming Washington, D.C. suburbs filled them with excitement, a tangible milestone eagerly shared with family and friends.

In the following months, the Berstein's, led by Mrs. Berstein, embarked on transforming their new house into a home, albeit mainly financed through credit. Long hours lay ahead to repay their debts, but Brea remained optimistic, seeing it as an investment in their future. Despite the financial strain, she viewed their journey as integral to the American Dream. With Ted by her side and a beautiful daughter in their arms, she felt reassured in her decision to marry him, after all.

Their transition marked a significant social and economic transformation. Settled into their new careers and neighborhoods, their circle expanded, and loved ones celebrated their accomplishments. Approaching their mid-thirties, they seemed to have fulfilled basic human needs, including financial stability. This newfound security allowed Brea to prioritize self-care, a pursuit she had postponed while working tirelessly as a nurse. Ted was supportive of her goals, appreciating her efforts to enhance her physical appearance.

Brea's journey toward self-improvement included regular visits to nail salons and spas, mindful eating guided by calorie-counting apps, and a wardrobe overhaul. She invested in stylish attire and intimate *lingerie*, believing that her efforts would reignite her marriage mate's old flame. "I wouldn't mind turning Ted into my "sex slave if he can keep up! " Brea once joked with one of her girlfriends. For his part, like most men, Ted would surely appreciate her holistic transformation. With determination and a touch of allure, Brea aimed to keep their passion alive, recognizing that maintaining desire required ongoing effort and attention.

Brea finds herself in a waiting game, longing for a transformation in her husband, Ted. She yearns for him to exhibit more passion, to hunger for her in a way that ignites her desires. Like a determined fisherman, she spends her days gearing up for the catch, convinced that nothing can be said about her allure. She envisions a bond between them so strong it ties Ted to her like a lifeline.

With a hopeful gleam in her eyes, Brea contemplates the best fishing spots within their home, eager for Ted to explore every technique, especially the tantalizing art of bobber-fishing. She dreams of being consumed by his desire, craving his relentless pursuit of pleasure. But alas, patience is her ally as she waits for Ted to be driven by her set parameters.

Yet, despite her persistence, Ted remains unchanged, offering little return on her emotional investment. She can feel the tension in the air, the palpable frustration in her voice. Like a man faced with a looming threat, Ted reacts defensively, wrestling with the weight of Brea's expectations.

Brea tries to motivate him, hoping to spark a fire in his libido, similar to Normani's overnight transformation in the song "Motivation." She links increased financial stability with heightened sexual vigor, nudging Ted to preserve his masculinity by meeting her needs.

But Ted is burdened not only by the demands of his job as an IT manager but also by the stresses of modern life. The constant threat of cyber attacks and the relentless pressure to be "always-on" take their toll, leaving him depleted mentally, sapping his manhood.

Brea struggles with the harsh reality that her husband's waning sex drive is not solely a reflection of their relationship but also a consequence of the world they inhabit. In this liberated era, where sexual freedom reigns, who remains untouched by the relentless pressures of modernity?

An ancient Hebrew proverb correctly says, "Hope deferred makes the heart sick." And sour it did indeed, as she found herself coping with frustration that simmered beneath her skin. Weeks had passed with a restless longing that Ted, her husband, seemed unable to match. His energy flagged in the face of her passion, leaving her to yearn for more than he could provide. "No substitute," she lamented silently, feeling the weight of unmet needs press upon her.

Financial worries had briefly diverted their attention, but now Ted's demanding career cast a shadow over their intimacy. Throughout their relationship, she had grown accustomed to Ted's subdued libido and sparse advances, resigning herself to a quiet longing that bordered on delusion. Yet beneath the surface, desire bubbled like a dormant volcano, restless and unfulfilled.

Upon learning the root of Ted's struggles in the bedroom, Brea knew a mental shift was imperative to ease the tension in their marriage. Like a vintner tending to her vines, she sought patience and made adjustments, hoping for eventual fruition. To his credit, Ted met her efforts with openness, embracing therapies and stress management techniques in their quest for resolution.

But did these endeavors truly bridge the chasm of desire that divided them? Brea's cravings waned at times, yet she couldn't shake the feeling of placebo relief, akin to sugar-coated promises of improvement. And amidst this fragile equilibrium, the question lingered: would it last?

Meanwhile, life carried on for the Berstein family. The COVID-19 pandemic had stretched time, nearly two years since Ted's parents, Frantz and Kelly, embraced their granddaughter Aubrie and their son. Relocating to Sun City, Arizona, they awaited a reunion, vaccines, and boosters paving the way for Ted's planned visit with Aubrie during his upcoming vacation.

Brea's absence during the first week loomed over the reunion, a bittersweet reminder of her obligations at the hospital. Yet anticipation crackled on the West Coast as the Berstein's prepared for their long awaited guests, eager to spend some in-person quality time, after years of virtual meetings.

For the Berstein family, chaos reigned as Ted juggled work crises and last-minute trip preparations. Racing against time, he tackled performance issues at the office while scrambling to pack for his imminent departure to Arizona. With the scorching desert climate in mind, he needed to assemble a suitable wardrobe in record time. Meanwhile, his wife fretted over ensuring their daughter Aubrie was well-equipped for his absence, insisting on packing an array of clothes, snacks, toys, and essentials for the week-long separation. Facing Ted's resistance, only half of her meticulously planned provisions would likely make it into his luggage.

Amidst the whirlwind, Brea had her own trip to organize, frantically purchasing new outfits and mapping out activities for their vacation in the Grand Canyon State. As the clock relentlessly ticked away, Friday afternoon crept upon them, heralding the eve of Ted's departure. Sensing the impending separation, their intimate encounter was infused with a bittersweet urgency, as if trying to savor every moment together.

The night before his departure was spent in the cozy embrace of their favorite show, offering a brief respite from the impending separation. As the night wore on, they finally managed to get intimate, calming some nerves!. Dawn broke too soon, and amidst bittersweet farewells, Brea accompanied Ted and Aubrie to the airport. With hugs and kisses exchanged, Ted embarked on his journey, already feeling the weight of his impending absence.

As the plane soared towards its destination, Ted braced himself for the challenges ahead, both in the scorching Arizona sun and the emotional distance from his wife, albeit just for a week.

On her way back home, Brea couldn't stop thinking about the previous night. In fact, she intentionally flashed on the entire scene as if she wanted to keep Ted with her, even though, by now, he was cruising 36,000 feet above sea level. Things got so vivid, so real in her mind that it brought her instant physical' and latent pleasures, so much so that, for some few intermittent moments, Brea's mind was off the road! She was basically double dipping; but who would blame her? She was smiling and experiencing a warm, fuzzy feeling inside, deep. "Imagine what I would have Ted done to me if he were home when I got there…" she thought for a moment. At least, she wanted to share it with him but she can't due to a temporary restriction of modern telecommunications technologies. However, some thoughts have to be verbalized for one to stay mentally healthy! But to whom else could Brea possibly share such intimate emotions and feelings without the fear of being scolded?

Brea wasted no time connecting with her best friend, Wendy, via her car's Bluetooth. "Hey there! Are you back from dropping them off at the airport?" Wendy inquired eagerly.

"Busy as ever, just on the road now but not home yet," Brea responded, her tone indicating a mix of anticipation and restlessness.

Wendy picked up on the vibe. "Sounds like someone's already missing him! You're flying out to Arizona next week, aren't you?" she teased.

"Missing doesn't even begin to cover it!" Brea exclaimed. "He needs to be here when I get back. My body's been screaming it since the moment I said goodbye," she confessed.

Wendy gasped in mock surprise. "Oh my! What's going on?" "That's why I called you!" Brea revealed. "It's strange, but it's true."

"Stop keeping me in suspense! What's true?" Wendy demanded eagerly.

"Last night, Ted and I... well, you know," Brea began, then paused. "It was supposed to be routine, but driving home, it's like I couldn't shake it off. It was like the first time when we were teenagers. Isn't that weird?" she confided.

Wendy pondered for a moment. "Hmm... Could have been amazing, or maybe you just didn't get enough," she suggested playfully.

Brea chuckled. "Probably both, but definitely the latter," she admitted. "It's just... my whole body reacted in a way I didn't expect. Thank goodness I'm alone," she added with a nervous laugh.

"Wow, what now?" Wendy asked, one could send some concerns in her voice.

"First, a long soak in the tub with Epsom salts. Then, a quick nap before work. Ted's still hours away from landing in Phoenix, so that's the plan," Brea outlined.

"Got it. Let's hope that does the trick," Wendy replied as Brea pulled into her driveway.

"Home sweet home," Brea declared, a sense of relief evident in her voice.

"Good! Before you go, I'm hosting a little get-together on Friday. Pizza, movies, the gang's all coming. You're in, right?" Wendy pressed, knowing Brea's schedule was wide open without Ted around.

"Wouldn't miss it for the world. Thanks for the invite! Catch you later," Brea confirmed, ending the call with a smile.

Later, Brea woke feeling refreshed after a solid four-hour nap. She quickly prepared for work, debating whether to call Ted before leaving. Checking the time difference, she decided a video call was in order. Ted answered, weary but smiling.

"Hey, sweetheart! Just got to Sunny City," he greeted.

"Hi, love! Where's my girl? How was the flight? How are your folks?" Brea asked eagerly.

"We're all good. Aubrie was a trooper, and the flight was smooth. We miss you already," Ted assured her.

"Can I see everyone?" Brea requested, her heart swelling at the thought of her family.

Ted gathered everyone around the tablet, and Brea's face lit up at the sight of her daughter and in-laws. "Hey, my baby girl! Mommy misses you so much," she cooed, feeling a warmth spread through her as she connected with her loved ones across the miles.

After exchanging pleasantries in the living room, Aubrie opted to stay downstairs with her grandparents while Ted headed upstairs to continue his conversation with Brea. Curious about how he was handling the weather and his plans for the week without her, Brea inquired. Ted expressed his intention to rest, spend quality time with his family by the community pool, and assist with household tasks while eagerly awaiting her return. Pleased with his response, Brea then playfully recounted an intimate moment they shared on her journey home. Ted, touched by her sweet gesture, expressed a longing to be together in the same location. They bantered affectionately before Brea, mindful of her impending work schedule, checked the time on her smartphone. Realizing it was nearly time to leave for work, she informed Ted of an upcoming gathering at Wendy's on Friday, to which he readily agreed. They bid each other farewell virtually, with Brea requesting a call before bedtime, and then signed off.

Relieved that Ted had arrived safely, Brea messaged Wendy to update her, maintaining their regular communication routine. However, despite her efforts to refocus on her responsibilities, Brea found it challenging to fully immerse herself in her work while separated from her loved ones. Nevertheless, she gathered her belongings and drove to her 12-hour shift at a suburban hospital near Washington, D.C., a routine she would repeat for the next three days.

As someone familiar with the grind of the American Dream, Brea found herself caught in the usual cycle of work, minimal rest, fleeting moments of relaxation, and the relentless pursuit of domestic bliss. The week passed swiftly, culminating in Friday morning, during which Brea deliberated over her attire for Wendy's pizza party later that evening. After settling on an ensemble that balanced strength and sensitivity in her mind, she set out for Wendy's, determined to embrace whatever the night might bring.

During her journey, Brea pondered various scenarios while receiving a text from Wendy confirming her arrival. Upon reaching Wendy's street, Brea noted the presence of familiar vehicles and remarked on the seemingly modest guest list to herself. As she approached the front door, Brian, a friend of Franck's, greeted her warmly and ushered her inside, his attention noticeably captivated by her presence.

Inside, Brea exchanged greetings and embraces with the other guests, engaging in light conversation about topics ranging from social media to weekend plans. Wendy, the gracious host, took orders for pizza before leading everyone to her entertainment room in the basement, equipped with a state-of-the-art TV and sound system. Despite initial seating adjustments to accommodate everyone comfortably, not everyone was entirely satisfied. Observing Wendy's diplomatic efforts, Brea mused about seeking "protection" in the absence of any real danger as she savored her wine and settled into the evening's festivities.

The conversations initiated in the living room seamlessly continued from where they left downstairs, with new topics sparked by the change in environment. Amidst the lively chatter, the doorbell interrupted, prompting Wendy to announce the arrival of the food spotted on her mobile screen. Franck enlisted Brian to assist with bringing the food downstairs, followed by a trip back upstairs for more drinks as the group began to indulge. The allure of the food and beverages prompted some to abandon their initial seating, standing near the refreshments or settling on the carpet in front of the TV, while others remained on the couch. Pizza preferences varied among the group, with some favoring different chains while others were just thrilled to be there. Brea, however, enjoyed pizza regardless of the source. Amidst the culinary exploration, the room buzzed with heightened energy and noise, perhaps fueled by the Enteric Nervous System's influence on mood.

By around 8 PM, everyone appeared to have satisfied their appetites, returning to their original seats after a few trips to the bathroom. The group deliberated between movie choices, including "The Adam Project," "Pride and Prejudice," and another romantic drama. As decisions were weighed, Brea attempted to reach her husband in Arizona to no avail, opting for a text update instead. Meanwhile, individuals reviewed synopses on various devices, ultimately favoring the second option. Liz's enthusiastic endorsement piqued Brea's interest, igniting a flurry of anticipation and inner conflict. As the lights dimmed and closed, captioning activated per request, they commenced streaming it, enveloping the room in hushed anticipation.

Midway through the film, tension mounted, heating the atmosphere as viewers were captivated by the unfolding drama. Sensing a need for respite, Brea confided her discomfort to Wendy before excusing herself to the upstairs bathroom. Meanwhile, Brian strategically positioned himself, attentive to Brea's movements, with an awareness of the power of proximity in social dynamics. Dressed in dark pink jeans and an elegant burgundy blouse, Brea unwittingly drew Brian's focus, prompting his subtle maneuvering to remain close by in accordance with the unspoken laws of social interaction.

Brea felt like a ticking bomb, ready to explode. The intense atmosphere of the basement, fueled by scenes from the movie, only added to her distress. It was like pouring more lava into an already overflowing volcano. She was burning up inside, feeling like molten magma. Despite knowing her bag held nothing to help, she headed upstairs to the ladies' room. She knew there wouldn't be any relief there either. What she needed was out of reach. Brea was desperate. After quickly freshening up in the ladies' room, she returned to the basement, not wanting any of the girls to see her in such a vulnerable state.

Brea felt really exposed. She bumped into Brian in the hallway on the ground floor as she was heading back down to the basement. "Oh Brian...!" Brea burst out, her voice trembling like Andy's wife, Gaelle, during that stressful Thanksgiving scene in "Scent of a Woman." "I'm sorry... I didn't mean to... I just wanted to see how you were doing. Are you alright?" he asked. "That's kind of you. Thanks. I'm... well... OK...! But I need to tell Wendy that I'm leaving." "You're leaving now? I wish you wouldn't...but if you must go, I can drive you. Just to be safe," Brian offered. "Really? Are you sure? I was feeling a bit dizzy before. But I think I'm okay now. You'd do that? Thank you." After saying this, she went straight to the game room to let Wendy and the others know she planned to leave.

In the basement again, Brea found herself in a charged atmosphere. The "movie" was still playing, but nobody was watching it anymore. They had moved on to other activities. For instance,

Wendy and Franck were no longer just watching in the game room; they were lost in their own intense moments, shooting their own scenes! Liz and Ricky were outside on the deck, lost in their own world, cruising in the Charm City Tunnel. And Donna and Jeff, well, she could hear them from afar, diving into their own adventure! Realizing Wendy and everyone else was in no position to talk, Brea signaled Wendy she'd call her later. Then, quietly and slowly, she returned to the ground floor, where Brian, the twenty two year old, was ready to drive her home safely...

Brea's exhaustion from the movie's emotional onslaught weighed heavily on her as they embarked on the journey. Brian's playful banter provided a fleeting moment of levity, distracting her from her turmoil.

She had selected her address from her car GPS to spare herself from having to provide Brian with step-by-step verbal directions. He then drove off from Wendy's street toward the Berstein's. Her house was about twenty minutes away, according to the GPS. By then, it was a few minutes past ten in the evening.

Looking at her demeanor, "How severe a punishment are you expecting when you get home?" he jokingly asked her to lighten her mood a little. And it worked! "LOL! None …! she said with amusement. Ted, my husband, and Aubrie, my daughter, have been visiting my in

laws in Phoenix since last week. I'm supposed to fly there the day after tomorrow to join them for another week and to spend time with my parents-in-law. So, geographically, if a spanking … should be expected, it wouldn't be from Ted, right? What about you, Brian? How come you are still out? Isn't past your bedtime," she said to him while looking at her smartwatch to tease him.

"You're probably right, 'Mom' unless you're ready for a digital sexcapade from your man tonight! As for me, I'm done with curfews. I'm a senior at UMD and have been living on campus for nearly four years. But, for the sake of argument, Imagine I've stayed out past curfew tonight... What would you do to me if you were acting in loco parentis? " He asked, feeling confident he was onto something.

"A dipping from who…? I don't know what you have been studying at your school, Brian. But, as far as I know, not all wildfires can be extinguished by dropping water or fire retardants at a distance from planes. Quite often, in order to be effective, many wildfires require that the firefighters, with their... *uhm* ... erected hoses, be exactly where the fires are raging, right?"

"What about you? How would you fight 'blazing fires ...,' Brian? As for what I would do to you. If I were ... well, it all depends ... The punishment should always fit the crime. And also depends on what you made up, right? Thus, tell me, how much heat could you handle? Could you really stay in 'the kitchen' when the heat has been on for a while...? How about baking a pie in the preheated oven without mittens?" she asked him rhetorically.

By then, both of them have been fully baked up in lustful desires and mental foreplays. That covert hypersexual and flirtatious conversation rekindled the same sensation they both experienced in Wendy's entertainment room, though, with a significant difference—they were no longer several feet apart, and her primal fear went up in smoke! Oh, how they both hated that seating arrangement, but protesting would have been a little too brazen then, especially for Brea! It was just not fair to them at all! "Please turn on that street for a second. My neighborhood is next. Now, let me drive, and please go and lay low in the back seat just for a moment. Do you mind? There are more tints at the back windows. My neighbors know that Ted is out of state ...," whispered Brea before Brian could even reply. As Brian processed all her loaded words' meanings, the whole car became intolerably hotter!

When Brea turned into her street, she was mainly on the lookout for any of her neighbors who might still be up. Some had their lights on, but she couldn't see any silhouette on the horizon. So she remotely pulled her garage door open, and to them, it felt like it took an eternity for it to go back down after she parked the car! What a relief for her! However, realizing what was going to happen, her heart rate went off the roof! But sooner than later, lust would probably win again! Time and again, it proved to be the strongest! She smiled dangerously when she remembered the child safety lock was on, trapping Brian at the back of the car!

That should have been a moment of illuminating reflection, one to ponder over the dire consequences of her next moves. For example, would it be wise to be so reckless with her marriage that she and her husband had worked so hard to build up? Would getting intimate with that young man do to her self-respect? What about her husband, does he really "deserve" such humiliating treatment? Being intimately involved with a third party? Period. In his own house? How would such treacherous behavior square off with her sacred vow to cherish her husband? Would he ever recover from such a treatment? And how would it be compatible with her belief in God?

Unfortunately, les carottes étaient déjà cuites! She wasted that crucial moment where she could have arguably taken one of the best decisions in her entire life by having that heartless young man Lyft® away to wherever he belonged to! But it didn't happen …and Brea ended up making the worst decision of her life, one that would have such a devastating dominoes effect for all involved. She let him in and then profaned her conjugal bed! And what for?

At 2:00 AM, Brea awoke beside a still-sleeping Brian, feeling thunderstruck by her nightmarish situation. Quickly donning her clothes, relieved that her compound migraine had subsided, and only then she began comprehending the moment's gravity! Waking Brian up urgently, she handed him his clothes and guided him to the basement bathroom for a shower. Returning with fresh essentials, she instructed him to wait downstairs once he was finished. Amidst her actions, she brainstormed fervently, addressing the immediate need to discreetly remove Brian from the house to avoid arousing suspicion among her neighbors.

Contemplating her options, Brea grappled with whether to proceed with her planned vacation with her husband in Arizona or confront the complexities of her marriage by either confessing to Ted and seeking forgiveness or initiating divorce proceedings. Alternatively, she entertained the notion of maintaining her clandestine affair alongside her legal commitments.

I would tell Brian that he couldn't stay here overnight. I would have him lying down on the back seat as I will leave the house until we are completely out of the neighborhood. Oh no! What if our neighbors, like Terry, Ted's good friend, had seen me leaving my house so early, even though none had seen Brian? Wouldn't they tell Ted? Maybe I could tell my husband it was a work emergency? Would he believe me, knowing they knew that I was on vacation? Do I really need to get him out of the house tonight? ... Unless I kept Brian in the basement as if we were in a temporary marriage situation, like the Muslim mut'ah or sigheh until I dropped him off Sunday morning on my way to the airport…, she thought while laughing. *But am I really ready to face off with Ted in Phoenix this weekend? Would I be able to act "normal" until I tell him the truth? Also, should things be over that quick with Brian unless I should divorce Ted for quasi-impotency or for whatever? And am I ready to live with sexual frustration for the rest of my life with Ted?* Her mind continued racing with such thoughts while she was showering upstairs. By the time she had left the bathroom, Brea had devised a scheme that mainly focused on the weekend. She gave no further thought to her future.

Despite all the thinking that took place in the shower, Brea's way forward was still pretty much foggy. Moments of lust such as those of the night before often shattered the basis on which lasting relationships flourished. They tend to create fresh tracks, new memory lanes, or even a powerful vortex that is almost inescapable. With her new lover in mind, Brea groomed herself there to please all his senses. Afterward, she wobbled her way back downstairs to the only 'real' person in her world at that moment in time—Brian! Once at the bottom of the stairs, she ran and jumped on him like it was her meeting with her husband after more than a week apart! If she loved two men, Brian was definitely the lone beneficiary here. After sharing her new plans for the rest of the weekend with him, they slept in the guest bedroom in the basement like it was their first time!

After that climactic night, Brea woke up by 11 AM, much later than usual. Looking at her phone, she saw that Ted had called her three times the night before she texted him before the start of "the selected movie" and twice that morning. So she rushed all the way to the second floor's master bedroom to call him back before he became wrongly dodgy. "I'll be back, Brian," steamily kissing him in between. Have to make a phone call upstairs," said Brea, still disheveled from earlier bedroom exercise.

"Hello Sweetie! How are you?

"I am so sorry that I missed your calls last night, but I called you three times afterward when I finally saw your text messages. I know it was a bit late...," answered her husband at the end of the line.

"Hi, Love. How is my girl? How are Dad and Mom?" she inquired further.

"We are all good here, love! The weather is much more tolerable than I thought. You know, Mom's cooking is still great. Aubrie and I have been having lots of fun at the community pool," answered Ted with excitement. "How was the party? Did you have a good time with the girls?" asked Ted to show personal interest.

"Yeah… We had! There were about a dozen people or so—lots of pizza and enough drinks. I caught up with Wendy and the girls, and then we watched "Dry…" a movie. When I got home, I realized that my phone was dead. I was spent! I wasn't feeling well, so I removed my makeup, brushed my teeth, and went to bed. I just saw your missed calls when I woke up in the middle of the night. I figured that you were probably sleeping. That's why I am calling you first thing this morning. I realized you were probably worried sick when you didn't get a hold of me last night before going to bed. Oh, baby! I missed you so much…," she pretended.

"Me too, Hon! I am glad you are well rested! We couldn't wait to see you here! Tomorrow is Sunday. Thank God! It couldn't come soon enough! Are you feeling better, though?" continued her husband, mildly anxiously.

"Not really … My whole body ached as a truck had run over it," she replied with a planned faint, dry cough.

"I am sorry, sweetie. I am not even there to take care of you. I was reading about your symptoms…Brea, do you think that it might be…?"

"Mmm…That's what I was thinking, too, babe. Just the day before... That's so unbelievable! I wanted to take the test this afternoon since you no longer need an appointment. Do you think I should go ahead with it, babe?" asked Brea.

"I am sorry, love! Yeah, there is no harm in knowing, right? Let's hope that it's nothing, OK?"

"Of course! Thank you, sweetie. I better get ready. I will call you later when I get the test result. I love you, honey. Kisses to my girl and all!" said Brea as she hung up the phone.

"Whew!" a relieved Brea said after she finally got rid of unsuspected Ted, seemingly without raising any suspicion. So far, her shower scheme was working: having a lustful weekend with Brian while she kept baking up Ted in a soup of lies! So she rushed back to the same basement room where she had left her lover earlier.

"Did you miss me … or are you hungry…?" Brea asked Brian flirtatiously as she was rubbing herself to him.

"Both! But now I am, foremost, literally famished. I haven't eaten anything since last night!"

"True! I have been so focused on my own needs… all along. Right away, though, I will fix you something upstairs, and then I should go 'tested… for …Covid or something' because I tricked Ted into believing that I might be infected so I could get wasted this weekend instead of just enjoying a one-night stand..."

"Wait a minute! How did you do that? Did your 'husband' fall for it? So you are no longer flying out tomorrow?... Meaning our weekend is just getting started?" Brian mused, his tone rhetorical.

"Yes, yes, and yes to all!" Brea replied, bubbling with excitement as she made her way up to prepare something for him to eat.

After Brian had eaten his fill, he turned to Brea and proposed, "Now, shall I properly 'test' you at my personal 'Women's Care Center,' a.k.a. my dorm room?"

"How good a physician could you be? Would your 'test regimen' be 'patient-friendly,' or would it involve any kind of 'pain' and "whole lotta probing?" She inquired with a playful air.

"Nothing that you wouldn't be able to handle, right? It would all be in good fun… and perhaps a little pain," he teased.

"Didn't I get a taste of it in the garage… And what a relief to hear that you actually have a home after all!" she joked.

"I am no gypsy!" Brian retorted, displaying his dorm room keys proudly.

"So I better get ready at once for the visit… right, 'Doctor B'?" she quipped.

"Yes, mom!" he responded, playing along.

After a brief interval, Brea descended to the living area where Brian awaited. Her lips were fiery red, and her busts were erect like drawn swords in a plunging neckline blouse. Success! Brian got the message and intimately kissed her. "Still hungry…?" Brea teased.

They exited through the side door in the kitchen, intending to leave the same way they had entered the previous night: she would drive while

Brian remained concealed in the back seat under cover of tinted windows. As they headed to the garage, Brea experienced a flashback, a sensual memory of the intense pleasures her backseat passenger had given her the previous night. Once again, fiery desires surged through her mind and body. She smiled at the recollection, but her daydream was interrupted by a text from Wendy. "What's up, girl? Still alive?" Wendy's message read. "Wendy! Girl! Oh! Yeah! I am alive and well! I am heading out just now. So can I call you later?" Brea quickly replied before pulling out of her garage.

"Hi, sweetie! How is my girl and everyone else doing? I am on my way to the 'pharmacy.' I will call you after I am done with the 'test,'" Brea texted Ted as they left the driveway. Those were true words of lies and deceit, indeed! She drove with him in the back seat until they were far away from her neighborhood. Then he took the driver's seat while Brea moved into the front passenger's seat, and they continued on their way to Brian's 'pharmacy' – essentially his 12-foot wide by maybe 15- foot-long study and sleeping cave for over three years. "On a beautiful weekend like this, lots of students attend parties near or on campus or at neighboring campuses," Brian informed Brea as they approached the campus. "Don't we have better things to do…?" she said with a sensual undertone, to which he smiled in agreement.

It was a Saturday afternoon full of excitement for both occupants. No longer in the shadow of her neighborhood and having any driving responsibilities, Brea started to imagine what Brian's dorm would look like, and there, envisioning quasi-unlimited and unrestricted pleasures. "I couldn't wait to get fully "tested"...! As for Brian, he could hardly keep his eyes and right hand off her! They were madly attracted to each other, and none could get enough of the other.

As Brian was finally preparing to turn onto the campus, another driver had lost control of his car, veering toward them and hitting their car head-on! Onlookers and passengers screamed at the top of their voices to avoid the unfolding collision but to no avail. It was a terrible accident. Other drivers and passers-by rushed to pull injured folks out and provided some first-aid until ambulances could arrive. But, unfortunately, both Brian and Brea had died on the spot, minutes away from their destination.

Who said that people should follow their heart? If only we all could behave in line with that principle: "Lust tends to be short-lived because, ultimately, everything is doomed to end." Moreover, did their story also highlight the wisdom of monogamy and marital fidelity?

"Brea's lust was in her skirts.

She gave no thought to her future.

Like laboring ants during Summer time,

with determination, her heart pursued it

Stranger had seen her nakedness.

And has laid hands on all her treasures...

In an untimely death, she has become powerless."

Chapter 7
Finding A Pearl in Irminger Sea!

"Marriage is the graveyard of passion." This idea had haunted Ai for as long as she could remember. She despised it because she had seen firsthand how it tore her family apart. Her father, Joe Davis, had once seemed restless, seeking an escape but ultimately resigning to a slow decline. He drifted away from his wife, Aika, spending more time with friends and growing distant at home, offering endless excuses. Aika tried to understand, but Joe remained defensive, like a wounded animal. As teenagers, Ai and her siblings reached out, trying to ease their mother's pain even though they needed support themselves. "Your dad now isn't the man I fell in love with," Aika often lamented to Ai, reflecting on their college days.

Ai's perception of marriage was deeply influenced by her parents' troubled relationship. Growing up, she witnessed the gradual erosion of affection and intimacy between her parents. Once vibrant and engaged, Joe became withdrawn and distant, leaving Aika to steer the difficulties of their relationship all by herself. Despite her efforts to bridge the gap, Joe remained elusive, deflecting inquiries with practiced defensiveness. This emotional distance took its toll on the entire family, prompting Ai and her siblings to seek solace in each other's company. However, even amidst their struggles, Ai couldn't shake off the profound disillusionment she felt towards the institution of marriage.

Forty years ago, love and life intertwined when they crossed paths in a college physics class. Their hearts brimmed with affection, making them inseparable on campus. They were "Bonnie and Clyde" amongst their classmates. Following graduation, Joe and Aika tied the knot, Joe proving himself a devoted spouse. Aika reminisced, "He made me feel like the center of his universe among other girls vying for his attention."

The memories invoked strong emotions in Ai. "Mom endured so much," she often mused, recalling her mother's emotional turmoil, deprived of essential affection and left feeling neglected. It left her bewildered and desperate, seeking solace in work and books. Ai and Chris grew up in this household, inevitably shaped by their upbringing. How would this influence their adult lives?

Ai was determined to carve her own path in life. She was adamant about avoiding the stagnant relationship her mother endured. "To choose rather than to beg" became her mantra. Following this creed, Ai aimed for financial independence, intending to carefully select her future spouse when the time came. Post-high school, she pursued a law degree in college. She crossed paths with Alex, a real estate management student in law school. While Alex found himself drawn to her, Ai remained steadfast in her commitment to her studies. Nevertheless, Alex's persistence was unsurprising to anyone familiar with Ai's allure.

When they were seniors, Alex and Ai didn't have many classes together anymore. So Alex had to wait for Ai after her classes or go to the library to talk to her. One Thursday afternoon, Ai was studying for her final exams with Sandy, one of her girlfriends, at the library when Alex noticed them in a study room at the back. He waved to get Ai's attention, and she smiled, which he took as a sign of welcome. "Here comes Alex. He's been asking me out for ages!" Ai said to Sandy as he approached them. "And...? He doesn't look too bad," Sandy replied. "I don't know!" Ai said with a smile.

"Hey, girls! I hope I'm not interrupting," he said politely. "It's cool!," they both chimed in together. Sandy pointed to the glass windows. "There's my ride! Gotta go!" She hugged Ai and waved Alex goodbye.

Alone with Ai, Alex looked visibly happy. "What's up? You suddenly seem optimistic! What did I miss?" she asked him.

"Well... happy being with you! How has your day been so far?" Besides, I rarely get this kind of opportunity when I can be with you alone and talk about *you*. They both chuckled.

Naturally, "Why?" would have been the logical reply, but Ai postponed it to satisfy Alex's curiosity while acknowledging his interest.

"Well, I didn't work today. So, I woke up late this morning and rested well. Then, I went to my taxation class. Afterward, I grabbed a bite at the cafeteria and met Sandy here to study a bit for our upcoming finals. That's my day in a nutshell. And yours?" she asked.

"I'm glad you got enough rest! You look superb! As for me, I had to work, unfortunately. But I didn't have any class today. I met with my group to finalize our commercial property management project due next week. Then I came here… looking for you," Jim explained.

"Your day wasn't too bad, after all. Here I am! Now you have my attention!" Ai said gleefully.

"I tend to be happier seeing that you're content! Although we've talked countless times over the years between classes or study sessions, to me, you still remain almost as mysterious as the first day we met. Is it by design, or do I need to do a better job?" Alex pondered.

"Alex, is it another one of your covert ways to ask me out? I'm just kidding! People tend to dance to the tune of the music that's playing, right? So, I guess you could do a better job! Is it too late to change your major? Perhaps becoming a lawyer instead of a real estate manager could have been useful, wouldn't it?" Ai teased.

"I would... if only you would accept to become my lifelong 'mentor'...! What would you say?" Alex wondered.

"That idea raises too many questions! Aren't you afraid of the unknown? How could you be comfortable putting all your eggs, your future, in one 'mysterious basket'?" Ai asked, probing his thoughts.

"That's my dilemma! He continued. The bigger the risk, the higher the reward, right? Therefore, although I would not say that I like gambling, sometimes, depending on the nature of the relationship one aims for, life doesn't offer any other acceptable alternative."

"Interesting! But if we're on the same page, why not consider other options? People should always have choices, right?" Ai prodded, hoping to understand his motives.

"If someone's planning an important transatlantic trip with a fixed deadline, and their airline might cancel or hike up prices, it seems simple, right? They could just choose another airline. But what if that airline has a monopoly on the route? What alternatives does the traveler have then?" Alex asked, trying to get Ai to open up.

Ai appreciated Alex's effort with a smile. "Maybe a permanent mentor isn't necessary after all! I like that last point," she said.

"Objection!" Alex joked.

"Overruled!" Ai played along. "Let's get back to your example. I'm not trying to restrict anyone from flying wherever they want. But airlines have to ensure passengers don't pose a threat, right?" She extended.

"Firstly, I really understand where you're coming from. Secondly, it's a relief knowing I'm not on your 'No-fly list.' Did I understand that correctly?" Alex asked, trying to gauge his standing.

Ai smiled again. "Did I really say that, or did you hear what you already had in your own mind? Maybe you're on it, maybe not. But why? Is it a background issue, or do I need to update my databases? Or both? Are you trying to fly under the radar, like some did twenty years ago?" Ai asked seriously, putting pressure on Alex.

"I believe in one God, but I'm not an extremist. I desire to travel with you and enjoy both the journey and the destination together. Ever since I met you, Ai, that's been my hope. Have you ever considered it, even for a moment? If not, could you later?" Alex pressed for clarity.

"Alex, who would choose swimming over flying first class? Nobody, right? So I understand your desire. The real question is, do they meet the conditions? And since people lose interest quickly in what they have because they fail to put in the required effort to appreciate it long-term. I can guess your answer or answers, knowing your infatuation. But are you genuine or just distracted by shiny things along the way? I've been around, Alex. So, believe me, if you will, like you, I have my own dilemma," Ai confessed finally.

"I made similar observations, Ai. Rest assured that I feel the same way. Any serious girl should do what you have been doing—asking, probing, and doing their due diligence to find credible information about any potential life partner. And now is the most appropriate time to do this before our hearts blur things up, right? Those decisions tend to impact the concerned parties in one way or another. May I ask you a personal question, though? Have you been involved in any way in any aircraft accident?" Alex asked her with hesitation in his voice, unwilling to open any Pandora's box.

Sensing his qualm, Ai shook her head negatively and then lovingly tapped his hand while finally throwing a bone his way. "No need to fear, Alex. Your question is most welcomed; I am not fond of taboos too much. We should be able to communicate freely and openly because lies and deceit tend to corrode the very fabric of a good relationship, don't you agree? " she rhetorically asked, trying to make him comfortable.

That time, it was Alex who sustained a hopeful smile while naturally shaking his head in agreement. But before he could muster up a word, Ai continued to finally answer his original question, this time directly with an explanation. "No! I was never involved in any literal airplane accident, but I doubt it was what you had in mind anyway. I got you, though. However, professionally and personally, I have firsthand experience with airline disasters and family tragedies. My life's mission has been to ensure that the airline industry pays a hefty price when it fails to do its due diligence to avert preventable accidents.

…On the other hand, the failure of my parents' marriage still has its impact on us. That's why I am also determined to do all I can so that what happened in Mom's marriage never happens to mine if and when I get married. Mom, Chris, my brother, and I paid woefully from Dad's post-matrimonial anhedonia …, she openly confessed.

"I am deeply sorry, Ai, for what you and your family had gone through. May I ask what happened?" said Alex in his then-new comforter-in-chief role.

"Mom met Dad while they were attending the same college. He swept her off her feet, so to speak. He was super romantic; he treated her like a princess. They were in love and spent most of their time together on campus. They got married right after graduation and went to Paris for their honeymoon. "l felt loved and desired when your dad and 1 were together, regardless of geography and our life's circumstances," Mom used to tell me.

…However, tying off the knot has changed everything for the worse, mostly for my mother. Unfortunately, her charming prince didn't survive the early, hellish years of matrimony. It broke him, indeed! Though he never left her physically, his heart or soul wasn't really there until his death. Her fond pre-nuptial memories were hardly enough to alleviate her post-matrimonial miseries. So, like flowers, love always needs a designated caretaker for it to last. So Dad, in becoming like a patán, has given up on his marital responsibilities with devastating emotional damages," Ai concluded after pouring out her heart to Alex. Afterward, she felt vulnerable and a bit relieved at the same time!

Alex listened attentively, absorbing every word Ai shared about her family's struggles and her own as a result of it all. He realized the depth of her pain and admired her courage in opening up. It was evident that Ai carried a heavy burden from her past, yet she faced it with resilience. As their conversation unfolded, Alex felt a stronger connection with Ai, recognizing her strength and determination. He knew that their bond was growing deeper with each shared experience. And in that moment, Alex made a silent vow to support Ai in any way he could, knowing that together, they could navigate life's challenges with unwavering strength and love.

In lending a sympathetic ear, Alex found himself facing a more significant moment than he had anticipated. Hearing such personal details from someone he was interested in was delicate. He knew he had to tread carefully, as one wrong move could jeopardize his chance with Ai. Feeling the weight of responsibility, Alex saw this as an opportunity to build trust, inching closer to a profound connection with her.

As he absorbed Ai's revelations about her family background, Alex couldn't help but wonder about the implications. Had he earned her trust? Was she opening up because she saw potential in him? These questions swirled in his mind as the announcement of the library's impending closure broke his thoughts.

Responding with empathy, Alex expressed his admiration for Ai's suppleness in the face of hardship. He reassured her of his willingness to support her, emphasizing his genuine desire to get to know her better.

Ai, in turn, expressed gratitude for Alex's understanding and patience, noting that she felt comfortable sharing with him in a way she hadn't with others. She hinted at the possibility of a deeper connection in the future, playfully suggesting they leave before being kicked out.

"Can I call you later... just to check if you get home safe and sound?" he proposed while they were still in the library's parking lot, determined to make up his bed.

Discerning the real intention behind that question, both smiled. She then shook her head positively before getting into her car.

Feeling a sense of accomplishment, Alex recognized the significance of their conversation. He appreciated Ai's depth and pliability, seeing her as a stronger person for her experiences. As they parted ways, Alex wished her well, feeling grateful for the opportunity to connect on a deeper level.

In this exchange, Alex and Ai navigate a delicate moment with empathy and understanding. Their conversation deepens their connection, laying the foundation for a potential relationship built on trust and mutual respect.

"Why, hello again! I hope that it's not a bad time!" she replied, being mindful of the time too.

"No, you're cool! To the contrary, the timing is just perfect because I have been nagging my brain to figure out the best time to check on you, as promised. I was just dazzled when I saw your face showing up with your call!" he explained how welcomed her call was.

"*Sweeeeeet*! I was doing the same but decided to do it before it got too late. I believe in equal opportunity in the matter of ... but did you say you have a picture under my name on your contacts? Probing Ai.

"Yep, I added it a minute ago! Are we cool, or would you like me to remove it? Proposed Alex, checking if he had made a *faux pas*.

"It all depends on how you do tonight, OK? I will surely let you know either way! Fair enough? Ai said to tease him.

"No objection! Tonight, I'm both happy and hopeful.

"Why?" Ai wanted to know.

"Because I feel that l am getting to know you better, well aware of my heart's desire at the end of that process. For me, after all, it's a thrilling prospect!" he replied with excitement!

"You sound clearly optimistic, Alex. Anyway, you know a great deal about me and my family. As for me, all I know is almost nothing about you, except where you go to school and maybe what you're majoring in ...

"Like yours, my parents have two children. My older brother James is 27, and I am 25 years old, born and raised in the house we now live in. But my brother lives now in Los Angeles, CA. We were raised very close to Dad and Mom, especially to my mom. They loved us. They refocused their professional lives when we were born, so one of them is always home after school. I am thankful for that. Here you have it," Alex added.

"Interesting upbringing! So you are both daddy's and mommy's little boy, eh? Ai continued to tease him.

"Maybe so. It has some upsides. For example, Dad taught me how to love a woman, and Mom, for her part, how a cherished wife behaves and sounds. As I am about to be done with college, I come to appreciate that insight more and more. What do you think might be a downside of a boy being close to his mom? Alex innocently asked her.

"Here, in the U.S., many kids would kill to have what you had. However, in any relationship, innocence can be both a strength and a weakness. It depends…Have you ever had a girlfriend?" she curiously asked Jim.

"Yep, l had one in my senior year in high school and the last one during my second year, but Julie dumped me after just six months for failing to meet her expectations," he confessed.

"Sorry, but l love your candor, though. But what did you want that she couldn't be? Or where did you fail her? Was it …bedroom related?" She said with a friendly laugh.

"Are you worried…I am just kidding! Seriously, my ex was a party animal; weekly clubbing was her thing. Though, at times, I would roll strategically for my woman, l was not ready to put myself onto such a destructive path. As for the second part of your question, l live for one day when you would allow me to help you gather in enough data to allow you to come up with your own verdict in line with this old Hebrew proverb: "Let someone else praise you, and not your own mouth; Others, and not your own lips."

What about you, Ai? Why does an alluring catch such as you remain single for so long? What couldn't you "fix" or tolerate from your last boyfriend?" Alex said with a certain confidence.

"Like you, Marx seemed to like my curves... But, unlike you, he couldn't handle the rest of the package. For example, he was often annoyed or went numb by any intellectual conversations. He loved sports. We stayed together for as long as possible because he was great in bed. But then I realized that although sex is a key part but not the whole thing in family life, physical communication alone was hardly enough to sustain any long-term relationship. So about a year ago, we decided to part ways on friendly terms," said Ai, ignoring Alex's fainting challenge.

"Thanks for sharing that with me. I am highly interested in knowing as much as possible about you, your desires, and your needs ... and wants. Would it be wrong to think that you might be a *bon vivant* or something like that? I am just being curious here," Alex tried to digest what he just heard.

"Alex, am I already sheepishing you? I would not say I like the sound of that expression, but all things being equal, I tend to hook on physical love. We live once! I want to be honest and direct as you have been with me so far. Alex, what about you, how do you love? Ai asked, wanting to press him on the issue.

"First of all, you are not scaring me at all. Second of all, l won't ever judge you! On the contrary, it is just another aspect of your personality that I can't wait to enjoy fully! So l think that you're going to love my open-door policy! Would I be able to fit the bill? You bet! I hope that answered your question. What does loving a man mean to you?" he wanted to hear more.

"Life's short. It's unpredictable. We, humans, are fragile and vulnerable. These are some of the things l learned from my parents' experience. Simply, I want to enjoy and be enjoyed by the man that I am gonna be with. In a nutshell, I wanna be rocked up in the cradle of love, all of it. I want someone who could perform a good 'tango session' until my toes curl. There are temptations everywhere in society; my philosophy is to satisfy my man fully in order to disincentivize him from looking elsewhere. Becoming his kind of honeypot should keep him around, right Alex? Like at Costco, the more house traffic there is, the more benefits there will be for all. Is there any flaw in my understanding?" she lightly inquired.

"Not in my good sense! Ai, you are truly a rare human being! I ... love you; Indeed, this has been my true feeling for you for years!" Alex finally uttered the three magic words, bypassing Ai's direct question.

They came at an unexpected moment! For him, it took her what felt like an eternity to react. Ai took that moment to piece together all the known, unknown facts mentally and weighed in her own feelings to see through the man at the end of the line.

"Oh! I love you way more, Alex!" She finally expressed her own emotions. By then, it was past midnight. But the call abruptly ended before he could utter even a word or react! However, within seconds, it was her calling him back, but that time, via Facetime for Alex's enjoyment! Ai wore a '32 degree' push-up bra and a V-neck tee. That was her way of officializing their upgraded relationship. But the heat radiating from all her smooth clothing failed to cover was enough to make him drenched! For her, it was a kind of warning shot or a window into things to come. His move!

He was tortured. She knew it. Alex could hardly concentrate to continue their conversation. "I wanna spend the rest of my life with you!" he said gravely. "Me too, " she replied.

They went ahead, talking about their plans for the weekend. Both had to work that Friday and study for their final exams on both Saturday and Sunday. Naturally, they made time for a romantic outing Saturday night in a downtown restaurant and went to see a movie that Sunday afternoon.

When it was almost one in the morning, Alex said to tease his new love. "Love, how have we been doing so far? Should I remove your picture from my contacts?"

"Absolutely not! I will send you some more pictures tonight, and dare you if you could use that as my caller identity. She laughed mischievously. And tomorrow, at the restaurant, I will select a better one to put on my profile!" she said with a serious tone.

"OK!" said Alex. They kept talking until she fell asleep, and Alex tried to hang up quietly.

"Love, you could barely stay awake while we were talking. I will call you in the morning. Sweet dreams. I love you." He texted her shortly afterward.

Come Friday, Ai and Alex talked at lunchtime but texted throughout the day with plenty of love and kisses emojis. "I will call you at 8 tonight," she texted him while leaving work. When Alex got home, he tried to do as much as possible before her call. Officially, their relationship was just a few days old, but they both felt like they had been together forever. Each day, like it is the case with all new burgeoning romantic relationships, they threw a ton of love and attention at each other!

As expected, Alex's phone rang, and the time on the math clock was 8:00 PM!

"My beauty! It was so hard for me to get you out of my mind all day today! How are you? How was work? Alex said after he answered the call.

"Peachy, but a bit miserable at times because you weren't with me, as expected. Truly, I am feeling great;

Ai, you breathe fresh air into my new life. Work is work. But since last night, we have an extra reason to work, right? " he enigmatically said

"I hear you! I feel the same way. Believe me! Are we thinking about the same thing?" he said, wanting to know the nature of the new reason that she just mentioned.

"Yeah … That's what I was thinking about! I am 24 and you are 25 years old. We are graduating this Spring. We have been working. Am I saying that we should go to the altar tomorrow? Maybe not, but, in the same vein, I am not going to put it up either needlessly, you understand? she reasoned.

"Agreed! Then, with that kind of timeframe, we have a boatload of stuff that we need to sort out. Do you know what l mean, *ma chérie*?"

"Of course! I know!" Ai replied.

That night, they talked past midnight, discussing at length about where their relationship was heading. They came up with a timeline for future milestones. They smoothed out their expectations and settled specific logistics questions. They agreed for him to move into Ai's townhouse after the end of formalities, although some renovations would be necessary. Alex wanted a bunch of kids, but she convinced him otherwise, at least for a few years, dangling all the potential extra benefits of a childless environment for the man of the house. Both were pleased with how their conversation went; both were surprised to see how natural it was for them to find reasonable compromise even on such delicate and essential matters.

"Thank you, my love, for being super reasonable," Ai said with a sigh of relief. Anticipating the topics of their conversation, she has decided to spare him the V-neck tee treatment. She wanted him to remain lucid, not feeling under any kind of feminine duress. And it worked!

"You're so welcome! By the way, I am so thrilled about our romantic outing," he said with audible excitement.

"Same here! I have found a Thai restaurant downtown that we can try tomorrow night. It has lots of great reviews. I just texted you the link. Got it? What do you think that it could work?" Ai proposed.

"Yeah! I look forward to being with you, regardless of the quality of the cuisine! For I am more curious about what you will be 'serving' tomorrow night…, especially *after* we are done eating dinner," Alex said mysteriously.

They both laughed shyly.

"Same here, love! But if the food happens to be good, the merrier the moment would be, right?" she added.

"Are you compounding ideas in my head …?" Alex asked rhetorically.

She then smiled complicitly.

Time passed, but nobody really cared. They both were overflowing with love and bursting with ideas they wanted to share! They just couldn't get enough of each other; fresh romance often craves everything to flourish.

While Alex was looking at Ai's last text, he noticed the time. "Babe! I can't wait for the formalities to vanquish once and for all the barriers between us. It's already past 1 AM. I have to finish a paper project for my real estate development class and study for my finals tomorrow …

"Are you ready to send me away tonight? Just kidding! You are right. We both need to do well in our final exams next week. So I understand. Have a lovely night, love! I hope that you see me in your dreams. I love you!" Ai said, sensing where Alex's head was.

"Oh yeah, my sweetest pie. By the way, I thank the heavens for my voiceless sheets lately!" confessed Alex.

And, flirtatiously, she kissed him goodbye. Afterwards, they both hung up.

Alex hoped Saturday would be the day when he could finally have some moments to put his eyes on hers! They have been friends for almost two years then. But it was going to be their first date since they were officially becoming boyfriend-girlfriends. As planned, he picked her up at half past six in the evening. He got out of the car to open the door for her. What did you expect? "One should always sing for his super," right? What wouldn't a man do for feminine intimacy? "Love, you look magnificent in this dress! Alex said as Ai was approaching his car. "Thank you. You look sharp, too, handsome," she replied.

They meticulously planned their outing, timing everything to secure a parking spot before arriving promptly for their 7:15 PM reservation at the restaurant. While some people go to events solely for enjoyment, for Alex, it is more about the company of others. He wasn't particularly interested in the menu offerings; Thai food didn't excite him one bit. He craved something more unique, something unlikely to be found on any restaurant's menu. However, his girlfriend, Ai, had already decided on her dish well before they arrived. So, when the waitress arrived with water and lemon, both were ready to order. Ai confidently chose her favorite dish, while Alex wasted no time requesting a Chicken Pad Thai.

"You were saying that your brother called you today. How is he doing?" Alex prompted her to finish up her thought that the arrival of the waitress abruptly interrupted.

"Yeah, right! Chris is doing fine. He was just checking on me as he regularly does; He knows that I hate taking exams. So he gave his usual prep talk and some tips. I told him about us. He was happy for us and said hi," she finally finished her reply.

"I am glad that Chris is well and you told him about us. I look forward to meeting him. I really enjoy talking with you. I was thinking about our last conversation and wanted to follow up on two things. First, you mentioned, among other things, that there could be some downsides of being close to my mom growing up; what did you mean?" he genuinely inquired..

"I really like that you listened when I was talking! Ok, yeah, though I was glad you experienced parental love throughout your childhood and got a good insight about romantic love from them. However, one possible disadvantage of being close to Mom is becoming too spoiled, or anyone too close to his mother eventually finding himself looking for his mother in his wife or a mother instead of a wife. I observe that spoiled brats tend to become overwhelmed by adulthood's basic responsibilities and are often ill-equipped to deal with life's basic challenges. Because of that, many of them tend to take refuge in drugs and alcohol to escape reality. I hope you understand where I am coming from," she sympathetically answered.

Before Alex could reply, the waitress finally came with their food. "Enjoy! Is there anything else I can help you guys with?" She asked them. Ai wanted a pink lemonade; however, Alex was still okay with his lemonade water.

"How is it? Do you like your food?" he asked her.

"It's great. I like it. And yours?" she then asked him.

"You can't mess up a Pad Thai! It's delicious! Let's get back to your concern. Shall we? My love, you are 100% correct about the potential danger of a spoiled kid. One of my mom's best friends had a son, Junior. His parents were well off. We went to the same schools when we were growing up. Junior was their Petit Prince, their only child. He drove an expensive car to high school, and he told me that, at home, he had quite a team of people always at his disposal to tend to all his needs and wants. But after graduating high school, he started abusing all kinds of drugs. At first, his parents try to cover it for him and to protect their reputation. However, Junior's substance abuse got so bad that they had to send him to rehab. As for my brother and me, our parents loved us, but tough love was often necessary. We didn't have a nanny. James was trained to help with taking care of me, and, as I was getting old, he passed that training to me to learn how to take care of stuff so he himself could get a break from doing it. Our parents made sure that we could take care of a house. For example, I did not particularly appreciate doing outdoor maintenance. But I didn't have any choice.

"On the other hand, Mom taught us how to cook and how to do laundry. So, believe me, I learned to love being useful in any way possible around the house. What about you? Would we need to hire a maid?" Alex asked jokingly to finish up.

"I am so proud of your parents, Alex. They seemed to do well with you. How much training did I get from my mom, especially? Well, I have been living by myself for almost three years. How do I look? But I will give you the same answer you gave me when I inquired about your work ethic compared to my ex; remember how cunningly you answered?" Ai said, striking him back.

"You look gorgeous! It's obvious that you know how to take care of yourself. But I remember that question well. I could have given you a theoretical answer, but would it hardly satisfy your curiosity? I doubt it. So, I wanted to be frank and not to be sly with you. However, tonight, we could kill two birds with just one stone—I could inspect your place to verify how good a job your mom has done with you and then provide you a practical answer to that specific question!" proposed Alex boldly.

"LOL! Wow! You are talking about being slick!" reacted Ai, a little bit surprised by Alex's daring proposition but trying hard to hide it.

"Babe, I have to run to the lady's room, she abruptly said. Excuse me, please."

She really needed a break. It wasn't just to use the bathroom, though. Her mind was thrown off by the gentleman's proposal at that moment. She worried about how her body's reaction might cause problems in public. And what would Alex think if he noticed? So, she had to get away from the table to gather herself in private. That's why she headed straight to the powder room.

While she was there, at the table, Alex was left with his own thoughts, wondering if its timing or his proposal itself was problematic. In fact, he even second-guessed himself about his own readiness for an eventual positive response from Ai. What about if she was offended by the way he talked? What does she think about what I think of her? Would she think that I took her for "*Une femme facile*"? Would that cause her to break up with me or to question my real motivation for wanting to be with her? "Here is the lady's drink! …How is everything? … Can l help you with anything else?" The waitress interrupted Alex's train of thoughts while still thinking about all of that. "What did you say?" Asked Alex after hearing her without listening.

"*While Ai was still in the powder room, first of all, she unsmudged herself and regained her composure; next, thinking about her eventual return to the table, she needed to come up with some kind of answer or counteroffer to Alex's frontal advance. Although momentarily I am troubled by Alex's escalatory offer, I realized that it stemmed from my insistence for him to provide more than a personal opinion on that problematic question. So what could he do? He probably felt boxed in. Since he couldn't emit any pheromones nor engage in some type of courtship display such as dancing, creation of sounds, and physical displays but had the same primal desires, maybe Jim just wanted to impress on my mind that he would be able to match, even beat my ex's performance in due time,"* she reasoned in herself. *"What am I getting myself into? He is probably anxiously waiting for a reaction. What can I do now to diffuse the tension we both felt after his bombshell overture?"* She laughed while looking at herself in the mirror. Finally, she decided to resort to the feminine form of 'escalate to de-escalate strategy' with the goal of smoothing things out once and for all. So all could save face.

Sitting alone at the table, Alex was still puzzled about how her new girlfriend would react to the audacity of his earlier bid. He felt an eternity had passed since she ran to the restroom. He wanted to check on her but realized Ai left her phone on the table. Gazing at the horizon, finally, he saw her exiting the lady's room and coming back toward him. For the first time that night, he was mainly focused on her luring face instead of her coke bottle figure, trying to decipher his own fate on it. He was not too good at facial interpretation.

Consequently, as Ai faintly failed to take her original seat, he thought his worst fear was about to materialize. Then, to his delight, she came to sit on… him instead!

"Ai, I truly like being with you…but the curious mind of mine cornered you earlier, right?" he raspily said

"Then you sounded like you could be ready for a demo, is that right?" she most sensually whispered in his left ear while intermittently sipping her pink lemonade, bringing all Alex's vital signs into critical territory.

"Same here, love! You are exactly where I needed you to be for the longest time! Yes, I was super anxious when you left the table. But all I meant was to assure you that you will be taken care of … But as for timing … I leave it up to you, even though the frame of your mind, well, nothing about you is conducive because I love them all," moaned Alex, as he felt like a woman who voluntarily accepted to go through a painful cosmetic procedure to enhance her beauty.

"I often sense that! How are you feeling right now, though?" Ai relentlessly and methodically puts considerable pressure on him.

"Oh yeah! It feels like l am being waxed up, a sensation of pain and satisfaction simultaneously! Ever since you are sitting on me, I am harboring grave thoughts, so grave they're hurting me a lot!" he finally confessed, Ai's spatial positioning, gestures, and tone of her voice having visibly taken a debilitating toll on the poor man.

"Does it mean that I am safe? Or do you mean that they are so grave that you want to hurt me, too? How much damage do you want to inflict on my body?" groaned Ai as she continued her onslaught.

"No to the first part, Oh Yeah, and yeah to all the rest! Believe me, my subdued crane, if permitted, has enough sustained power to build you up, to pump you, way up as to scrap your skies!" replied Alex as his closing argument, his torturer being also the judge!

As Ai spotted their waitress coming in their direction, she scrubbed herself off him to regain her original seat across from him. Gazing at her, Alex was as relieved as he was frustrated! The former because that put an end to the absolute agony that his woman had put him through as a price for peace... But the latter was due to the fact he felt like a hamster on a wheel: he burnt a ton of energy holding her so close but failed to produce any meaningful work. While the server was standing by the table, Ai asked Alex with amusement. "What would you like for dessert tonight, my sweet pie?"

"What I really desire is not on the restaurant's menu!" he answered cryptically. Bewildered, the waitress looked confused and asked him if she could help him find the particular pastry he was looking for. Ai smiled because she fully understood the subtext of his complaint but resolute in her heart, that night wouldn't be the one to serve him any horizontal refreshment as of yet. "We will share a Tiramisu, ma'am!" she finally ordered. Alex smiled while shaking his head in wonderment.

After finishing their dessert, they eagerly anticipated the server's return with Alex's card. While waiting, they probed into discussions about their future final exams and their aspirations for life after college. Both felt optimistic about their exam performance. Ai expressed her intention to continue working at her law firm and anticipated a promised promotion. Meanwhile, Alex aimed to secure a job more closely related to his area of study.

Once Alex signed the restaurant's copy of the bill, they exited the dining room. Despite Ai intentionally adding a bit of tension to the latter part of their evening, they both agreed it had been a delightful and intellectually stimulating night.

Romantic individuals often find themselves reluctant to say goodbye, preferring to prolong their time apart until they can meet again. Outside Ai's house, they shared a goodbye kiss while seated in the car. "Make sure to call me before you go to bed, all right, baby?" she asked as she prepared to leave the car. "Of course, my dear. You know I can't drift off without hearing your lovely voice," he replied, offering a compliment.

That evening, Alex's perception of his girlfriend underwent a fascinating shift: he discovered that she possessed a depth of character far beyond what he initially assumed. Rather than being prudish, Ai revealed herself to possess a refreshingly open-minded demeanor, striking a balance between sophistication and decency that captivated him. In his mind, she transformed into his very own Wonder Woman, a source of awe and admiration.

As he made his way home, Alex found himself lost in contemplation, relishing the stimulating company of Ai, reveling in her articulate expressions, and savoring the alluring scent of her presence. It was akin to stumbling upon a treasure trove of red and pink blossoms adorning his beloved's doorstep, each petal whispering secrets of anticipation and longing. Stooping to inspect them closer, his heart skipped a beat as he discovered a tender note left just for him, a silent invitation into her world.

"Love, no need to ring the bell," the note beckoned, "I've left a spare key beneath the doormat. I've been eagerly awaiting your arrival... Welcome!" With a sense of exhilaration, Alex willingly accepted the invitation, unlocking the door to unveil a scene even more enchanting than he could have imagined. The path ahead, strewn with roses, guided him towards a staircase adorned with delicate blooms, each step a testament to the anticipation hanging in the air.

His pulse quickened, and Alex's imagination ran wild, envisioning the possibilities ahead. Yet, amidst the floral symphony, a solitary garment caught his eye – a daring red feminine wear positioned provocatively on the stairs. "Does its color have any 'loaded meaning ?" he mused, his thoughts veering towards the tantalizing prospect of intimacy. It was a moment of rare closeness where desire mingled with curiosity, prompting Alex to reflect on the significance of this clandestine encounter.

"This moment," he whispered to himself, "is a testament to the privilege of intimacy, a delicate dance between desire and anticipation." With each step, he ascended toward the unknown, guided by the tantalizing clues left in his wake. At the top of the staircase, amidst a sea of roses, lay another note bearing a series of probing questions that tugged at Alex's heartstrings.

"Since you arrived at my doorstep," the note began, "what thoughts have occupied your mind? How do you perceive me now, in this moment of revelation? What stirred within you upon encountering this intimate token? And most importantly, in which of the many chambers upstairs do you imagine finding me waiting for you?" It was a challenge, a playful invitation to explore deeper into the mysteries of their connection, to navigate the labyrinth of desire with intuition as their guide.

Finally, Alex got home from his lovely dinner with his girl and found himself in an empty house, and cold! Everything was in his imagination! There were no lovely, erotic notes, no multi-colored petals-filled pathway leading to any ever-ready bedroom, and absolutely no hot, over-sexed feminine body waiting for him in any shape and form up there! Just an empty house! In fact, as a single man, he has found the house even colder than he left it after getting so baked up by Ai's risky moves at the restaurant and so consumed by so many lustful thoughts of his way home! He felt truly exhausted and ready to crash. And he did. However, in bed, he video-conferences with his girl. She was not in better shape, either. So they started talking, but both quickly fell asleep that night one after the other, with their phones unwillingly becoming their sleeping companions!

Like a man possessed, Alex found himself consumed by thoughts of Ai, each question propelling him further down the rabbit hole of anticipation. Yet, amidst the flurry of emotions, Alex realized because of the impending pressures of their final semester and upcoming graduation, he would need to cultivate unusual manly patience until his alluring girlfriend would eventually be in the mood for this type of love. He tried to savor his great moments with her, knowing that the path forward would be paved with hope and discovery.

Sandy's phone call woke Ai up that Sunday morning. They had a 10:30 AM appointment to study and finish a group project at her place. She extended her hand to snooze it while making a mental note to call her back on her way there. Then, stretching on the bed, Ai wondered what happened last night. "Hello, love! Are you up yet? What did you do to me last night …? I will call you shortly. Love," sending a quick bed text to Alex before hitting the master bathroom to start getting ready.

Her reflection in the bathroom mirror showed sudden anxiety on her face about the upcoming back-to-back exams. She decided not to linger on it too long. But she was definitely in a good mood about the direction of her romantic relationship and her upcoming college graduation. She was also pleased with the number on the scale and her curves, which confirmed that her intermittent diet coupled with regular exercise is working nicely. While under the shower, she mentally decided to wear something else instead of the outfits she had planned earlier, focusing more on comfort rather than on glamor. She heard her phone ringing. But whoever was calling had to wait since her phone was not waterproof!

Ai was the kind of woman for whom makeup isn't the usual strategic ally. Nature did things for her! So, for her studying session rendezvous at Sandy's, she barely wore any cosmetics but still looked stunningly gorgeous! A reminder that feminine beauty is, above all, symmetry! Her phone's clock indicated five minutes to 10:00 AM, so she ran to her downstairs living room, stuffed her book and study materials into her backpack, and headed toward the front door. As she was pulling it to lock it up, Ai realized that she had forgotten her keys in the kitchen! So she rushed back inside to grab them!

"On my way to you now," she hurriedly texted Sandy, giving her a heads-up just before she drove off. Afterwards, she commanded her phone: "Hey Siri, call my boyfriend!"

"Hello, my girl!" Alex answers through her car's Bluetooth almost instantly.

"Hi, You missed me, eh? I am sorry that it took me so long to call you back. It was one of my slow mornings," she said with some kind of apology.

"No worries, love. Same here! When are you supposed to meet up with Sandy?" he asked her.

"Actually, I am heading there now! Between waking up a bit late, thinking about us, and getting ready this morning, I didn't have enough time to call back either Sandy or you. I hope that she doesn't dramatize the fact that I texted her instead of returning her call!" said Ai, a bit worried.

"She shouldn't love. You have a good reason, and you are about to see her, right?" he reassured her. "By the way, knowing you both, are you guys up for some girls' talk, or are you really going there to study for the finals?" continued Alex.

"LOL! Probably a bit of both! But this time, I hope that it will be mostly the latter. We both need to do good in them. I will tell you all tonight. I promise," she replied with half of a concession.

"I am certainly looking forward to spending some time with you. Also, you mentioned something about 'innocence' the other day, and I wanna know what you meant when I see you tonight, OK? It's nothing to worry about; I said it now in case I forget again. But I want you to concentrate on your exam prep session with Sandy," he repeated to encourage her.

"Thank you, love. I appreciate it. But am I in trouble?" she jokingly asked with a smile. "What about you, Romeo? What you gonna do in the meantime?'" Ai wanted to know.

"'Romeo?' You never called me that before! But I kind of like the sound of it. Is its meaning as attractive as it sounds? Please know that, for a while now, it has been you who have given me real trouble, not quite the reverse, as of yet! But no worries! When that time comes, it will be good trouble.

On the other hand, Bill is coming over for our last study session for most of today. At what time will you be back home? When should I pick you up tonight?" asked Alex.

"Knowing you both, are you guys going to play video games, or are you going to study?" she sarcastically asked, flipping his initial question. "As for later, it makes more sense that I pick you up on my way from Sandy's house. Let's say 6-ish? That will give us enough time to grab a quick bite and catch the movie on time. What do you think, love?" she proposed.

"Great idea! The idea of you giving me a ride troubled me to the core! It has been my dream to be driven by you …Thanks, love. As for Bill and I, I hope that it will be mostly the latter, not the former! Just kidding! We need to do some serious study, just like it is the case for you and Sandy. I will surely fill you in later," Alex replied.

"Deal! Ai said as she pulled into Sandy's street. "Love. I just arrived! Kisses! Don't study too hard! I will see you later. I love you!" she said to finish.

"It's a pleasure talking with you. I love you, too. Let me know when you will be leaving,"

"We surely will do. Bye, love!" Ai said and then finally hung up.

"Girl, what's up! I am so glad to see you," the hostess greeted Ai as they hugged ever tighter.

"Same here, Sandy! Thanks for having me," she said gratefully. "Where is everybody?"

"My parents went to the mall with Matt. We're gonna be in the basement. We'll be alone there. Do you want anything?" proposed Sandy while leading the way.

"I am ok for now. How old is your little brother now?" inquired Ai.

"He is 11; he was late in the game, and mom didn't expect any more babies after me. Here we are; now we all love him so much," her host answered as they sat down at her study station.

"Life has never been one to embrace predictability. It's complicated mosaic defies the confines of a predetermined script; deviations, rather than exceptions, weave the very fabric of existence," she remarked in response to Sandy's discourse.

"Indeed, deviations need not necessarily connote abnormalities. Take yourself, for instance: in this moment, love radiates from every pore of your being. It's a joy to witness. Perhaps you didn't anticipate encountering it in this time and place, did you, my dear?" observed Sandy.

"Thanks, Sandy! LOL! Yes, indeed. The sooner people realize and accept it, the better they will fare under this Sun. If we are afraid of the unknown or tend to be allergic to life's fluctuations, we might be safe where we are, but we will never trail any new roads either. Right? So it's really up to us to decide what we want to learn from the passing of time! As for me, proper reflection on my parents' romantic failures and on my own experiences with Alex for the past two years have taught me that much," Ai replied.

"Good for you both! Alex has always liked you, but until recently, you have been apathetic to his feelings, inventing all kinds of reasons or excuses all along. I am curious to know what happened to them?" Sandy pressed her.

"I guess I was trying hard to project strength for self-protection then! After all, excuses were just that! So, I finally realized that hiding one's underbelly doesn't harden it nor make it disappear. On the contrary, the longer it remains hidden, the more sensitive and vulnerable it tends to become. So, the so-called fabricated obstacles you mentioned were only meant to be a means, not the end. Their role ended when I figured out that l could emotionally trust Alex. Since when does falling in love become a crime?" asked Ai with a laugh.

"Oh! Not that at all! I am happy for both of you guys! Believe me, I was purely curious. How is your relationship going? Do you feel it's just puppy love or that he might be the real deal? Or is it too soon to tell either way?" Sandy questioned.

"Thanks, girl. No, we are really in love. In fact, the other day, when the big "M" question popped up in one of our conversations, none of us wasn't sheepish about the idea at all. Surprisingly, we ended up discussing its planning comfortably at length. Isn't it a good sign of things to come?' Ai asked her with satisfaction in her voice.

"Wow Ai! It seems that you are ready to settle down! Does that mean you guys have done the matrimonial polka?" curious Sandy asked.

"You know, men! For them, it's the ultimate proof of love! Alex is surely no different! However, for the time being, Betsy remains uncurled! But, believe me, it's darn difficult to choose to be singed by burning desires when a nearby well-equipped firefighter couldn't wait to flux you in and out …! Sandy, when will we start studying?" an impatient Ai finally attempted to change the subject.

Ai and Sandy's conversation continued for the next several hours, talking about boys' and girls' stuff and their plans post-graduation while trying to do some studying in between until it was time for Ai to pick up her new guy friend for their movie night.

Ai called him unsuccessfully when she got into her car but left no voicemail. She decided to text him instead, giving her ETA to his place. On the road, she wondered if playing video games with Bill had caused Alex to forget their appointment. In any case, she reasoned that it was still safe to drive there since his house was on her way home, anyway. Moreover, Ai knows Philips, Alex's parents, but she is not yet sure if they are aware of the recent change in the nature of their son's relationship with her.

While she parked in front of the house, she double-checked to see if she got any message from Alex. Still nothing! When she rang the bell, it was Laurie, Alex's mother, who opened up the door. "Good afternoon, Mrs. Philips!" Ai greeted her with a broad smile.

"Ai, how are you doing? Please come in! What could I get you to drink?" she asked as she led Ai into the dining room.

"I am fine. Whatever you have would be fine! Thank you, Mrs. Phillips. I am just anxious about the finals this week. How are you and your family doing?" Ai asked.

"We are all doing just alright! Thank you, Ai. Alex is upstairs napping. Dan runs to the neighborhood beer and wine store to get us some wine for dinner," Laurie replied as she put a glass of apple cider in front of Ai.

"No wonder. Alex and I are going to see a movie at the theater tonight. I was supposed to pick him up on my way from Sandy's house. So I called and texted him before leaving but didn't hear a beep from him. That explains it! That's why I am here, knowing that he was supposed to be home studying with Bill," Ai said to justify her presence.

"I see. No worries. You are always welcome here. In fact, Bill left here about an hour ago, and Alex told me about his afternoon plan." I will take a power nap before Ai comes," he told me." Just a minute, my dear. Let me tell him that you are here," she proposed on her way there to wake him up.

"He said that he will be down in a minute," announced Mrs. Phillips after a few moments.

"Oh! Thank you," Ai said politely.

"Alex told us how much he is in love with you. Lately, we have observed that he is a little happier despite dealing with the stress of preparing for his final exams! You probably have something to do with it, is that right, Ai?"

She smiled, but they heard the front door open before she could answer. It was Dan, Alex's father. Ai stood up and walked toward him to greet him. "It's nice seeing you!" Mr. Philips said.

"Dan, aren't you interested in knowing what this girl has done to our son lately?" Mrs. Philips insisted on giving Ai another opportunity to opine on the matter of the day.

"Have you ever thought that it might be Alex who has done something to me? You have raised a caring young man, and I have been a beneficiary of your labor of love for two years now. Thank you! But to be honest with you, though, recently, the more we spend time together, the more attracted I am to him! In fact, it's a mutual attraction, and we made it official!" Ai finally answered diplomatically.

While the Philips' were trying to come up with an appropriate reply, all their attention suddenly turned toward Alex, who was finally coming down off the stairs to join them in the dining room. "I am sorry, love. I was more tired than I thought because I was fast asleep the minute I hit the bed after Bill had left," Alex said as he kissed his girlfriend.

"No worries! Your parents have been great hosts.' She assured him.

"You should stay and have dinner with us. What do you think, Dan?" Mrs. Philips proposed.

"Mom ...! We really want to catch the movie! We both have been trying for several weeks to find a time that will work for us. We won't have time for both, right?" countered Alex as he looked first at his watch and then in Ai's direction.

It was not hard to figure out Ai's preference. However, she refrained from expressing it, not knowing how his mother might interpret it. So, she decided to let her future husband handle that delicate situation. In the meantime, both interested parties kept going back and forth with arguments about why all should enjoy dinner with their guest rather than going out. It's basically a toss-up between mom and son at that point!

"In the direction things are moving, I guess we will have plenty of opportunities to break bread with AI in the near future. What do you think, honey? So let Alex arrange another more convenient time with his girlfriend to have her here for dinner. We can understand how insatiable new love can be, can't we? Therefore, let's have our romantic dinner here, alone," her husband proposed. Everyone was pleased with his insightful suggestion. So Alex thanked his dad and then kissed her mom goodbye. Ai followed suit, kissing them goodbye too, and rushed towards the front door where he was already standing, waiting for her.

Now, out of their view, Ai jumped on her boyfriend, kissing him, thanking him for bailing her out so expertly with no one getting unnecessarily upset. Alex didn't expect any of that from her, but nonetheless, such spontaneous gestures are always welcomed. When his mouth was free, he thanked her for her generous, romantic overtures and for her strategic patience and neutrality while trying to sort out how the night should end with her mom. "I was frightened, not wanting to say or do anything that could create friction between you and your family, especially your mom. I am truly impressed by your composure while sandwiched between two women you love; pleasing two women simultaneously is awfully difficult! But you did it nicely!" she continued praising him, but this time verbally.

"Thanks, love. Dad's suggestions at the end were very helpful. Please know that you can do what you did or anything else of that nature to me anytime, OK? No warning or pre-authorization will ever be needed!" he frankly suggested. They both laughed out loud.

"Oh yeah! You liked it that much! It feels like you are an insatiable man! Did l get that right?" she asked, wanting to peer into his intimate expectations.

"Oh! How I like the fact that we can talk about any topic at any given time! I am glad that you asked. However, now it's hard to provide an honest answer for at least two reasons: first of all, is it even possible for a man to be naturally insatiable? How would you even define it? Second, to properly judge someone's appetite, one would need to observe him eating where food is plentiful, available when needed, and the cost is reasonable. Do you understand what I'm saying? Do I need to explain myself?" Alex countered mildly, trying not to lose her at the same time.

"Let me see if I understand what you're saying. I remember an old Hebrew proverb: "One whose appetite is satisfied turns down even honey from the comb." I can see why. Once a man eats to his fill, his body always needs time to absorb the nutrients it needs and then completes the digestive process. Although the length of such a process may vary for each man, none can ever bypass it. So physically and mathematically, the man would run away even from something as delicious as natural honey during that time, regardless of how his wife has labeled him during the non-feeding season. Am I on the right track? As for the second leg of your argument, a wife needs to study the market, comparing the offer with the demand to get all the relevant facts before she can take or recommend corrective actions to keep her engine fired up on all its cylinders. Without such a deliberate approach, she will create artificial, unnecessary shortages with undesirable consequences. Since you don't yet know what I will offer, how much, how often, and at what cost, it's best, at least for now, to reserve judgment on your demand or appetite. Love, if I understand what you meant, I must admit that you may be right," she conceded amicably.

"As for myself, I have to admit that you read my mind!" Alex replied diplomatically to keep the channel of communication open.

"No, rather, I heard your heart! I guess that I might have focused too much on your 'symptoms'…!" she said mysteriously.

"My… 'symptoms'? That's why earlier you diagnosed me with …something. How did you call it again …? "MELAS …," Alex asked with a faint surprise.

"LOL! Yeah! You remember! " Ai reacted with more surprise.

"Man with Excessive Love for Ai Syndrome! Voilà! Are you saying that you finally have more data to develop a more accurate diagnosis? How bad is it? Do I need to stop the car now?" he asked her jokingly.

"Are you sure that I said that? It sounds more like an educated guess! In any case, your 'problem' is natural, not caused by poor dieting, lack of exercise, or anything like that. Also, you will not find it in the most updated medical diagnosis and treatment book. Your underlying symptoms point somewhere else," Ai replied with a serious face. "The following account could and further "consultation" help us come up with the correct diagnosis and prognosis."

Chapter 8
The Masculine Disturbance

"Denzel Lamont, a young man hailing from one of the vibrant South American countries, offers a fascinating glimpse into the fabric of his community. As the eldest of three siblings, Denzel resided with his parents, deeply entrenched in the daily rhythms of their lives. Across the street, the Lamonts shared a close bond with the Ferguson's, a family whose prosperity mirrored theirs.

Echoing the wisdom of an ancient Hebrew proverb that says: "When good things increase, those consuming them increase.", the Ferguson's, headed by John and Denise, experienced a bountiful increase in their blessings. Nestled amidst fertile farmland in the low plains adjacent to a vital river, their homestead flourished abundantly. The brood expanded to nine, comprising five energetic boys and four enchanting girls: Liz, Janett, Jennah, and Nadyah.

In the bustling complexities of their existence, the pursuits of youth held sway over Denzel and his peers. Amidst the vibrant mosaic of religious, social, and political currents, education, soccer, and romantic dalliances took precedence. European football, or soccer, emerged as the unequivocal passion, igniting daily matches that spilled onto the sun-drenched streets after school. Unfazed by the caprices of weather, enthusiasts reveled in the exhilaration of rain-soaked showdowns, infusing each encounter with the fervor akin to Champions League finals.

The presence of girls on the sidelines lent an additional layer of excitement, their spirited cheers mingling with the fervent cries of encouragement for brothers, cousins, friends, or paramours. As the twilight descended and the final whistle blew, weary yet elated players, Denzel among them, sought refuge on the Ferguson's welcoming front porch. The post-game analysis unfolded amidst animated discussions and boisterous banter, providing a vibrant epilogue to the day's sporting spectacle.

A visitor entering the Ferguson compound from the front porch would go through the living area, then through a hallway with the master bedroom on his left, continue through the girls' bedrooms on both sides, followed by the kitchen pantry area with a central back door leading into the backyard. From there, he would have seen the girls' shower on his left, next to a domestic water reservoir, and the boys' on his right-hand side, adjacent to the actual cooking area. Further into the yard was a seating area, followed by the boys' dining area with a door leading to their living quarters.

After each soccer game, Ferguson's living area served as the locker room for the boys' closest friends, such as Denzel, who preferred to take his shower with them officially for further discussion of the game, but in reality, it was his opportunity to stalking 18 years old Jennah whom he had a secret crush on when he was 16 or 17 years old. Because of his friendship with her brothers and two of her sisters, Denzel has almost unrestricted access to the house, enabling him to lurk around her whenever she was cooking, getting dressed, or relaxing on the front porch, but he had the courage to make his feelings known. After a few weeks, Jennah was pretty sure he liked her, even though it was just a telelove.

Proximity is a good ally of lust. And, like a drip of water falling on a rock, Jennah's feelings towards Denzel started to evolve from her initial indifference to curiosity. Though Denzel didn't know how to express his love for her, he managed to utter the three famous words one day after she asked him why he wouldn't stop stalking her. Even though, at first, his persistence made Jennah sometimes uncomfortable, then being aware of his intentions, she said to herself! 'I would rather be desired than be ignored.' How would she keep his hope alive? It's well known that a woman hates to feel guilty and responsible for a man's agony. So one afternoon, while Denzel was standing at the girls' quarter, Jennah came out from her bedroom and kissed him French style. She went so deep she almost tasted the back of his throat. His manhood reacted instantly and violently! "Ooh! It better not be a roll of quarters in your pants." She commented. No, but you don't need to ask. That was his first-ever kiss by a girl! Similarly, it was her first one by a boy!..

"That burgeoning relationship opened up Denzell's hanker box, she continued. Unlike the leopard seals of the Chilean Patagonia during the breeding season, surging hormones caused him to sing, even during the off-season. So he couldn't get Jennah out of his mind. He wanted to grab her, kiss her all the time. He wanted to do all kinds of stuff with her all the time! So they often went to a Cuban lady's house, who lived at the end of their street, to kiss and make out several times each week. But, at night, his sheets have proof of his regular men's dreams, surely inspired by her. During the day, he purposely downsized his underwear to avoid embarrassing moments! Denzel's mind was so tuned up on feminine matters that even seeing a woman's panties on a clothesline would have given him morning wood! Unfortunately, Denzel lived for many years with that condition!" Ai concluded.

"Oh my…! What was his problem?" a curious Alex wanted to know since he had been wondering if his girlfriend was describing him under a fictional Denzell.

"Denzell suffered from AVD or Acute Virginity Disorder! But you, love, may have a milder form of it,'" she said with a big laugh.

"I would love having you as my 'physician' all day long for proper treatment! Let's assume your diagnosis is correct. Is AVD treatable?" inquired Alex.

"Yep, but not by any conventional drug. In due time and with your cooperation, though, I could make available a natural remedy… that could prove to be very effective against your condition. Interested?" she asked to tease him.

Alex didn't say anything because he was too focused on his parallel parking maneuvers in a tight space near the movie theater. Then they rushed inside, having just enough time to get some caramel popcorn and drinks. Ai pulled out her phone from her handbag, and the attendant scanned both QR codes on their electronic tickets. Looking at his watch, Alex thanked Ai again for purchasing it online. They watched the West Side Story movie (2021 Version). She liked it more than he did. And that was just fine! He was never a fan of musicals anyway. He was mainly there to fulfill his boyfriend's duties!

Both agreed not to stay out too late that night because of their final exams the next day. She dropped him off at home after seeing the movie. "...I am super interested in your cure. I don't want to needlessly continue suffering as long as Denzell did," said Alex in response to her question. Ai smiled. " I know. I am with you. Let's get those finals and graduation behind us. Then we will focus on our future," she said sympathetically, and then he kissed her goodbye.

Chapter 9
The Official Announcement of the Storm

It's graduation season! Alex and Ai have another reason to celebrate. Their graduation ceremony took place in the middle of the Spring season. It was an important milestone in their adult and professional lives. Their respective parents and friends were filled with both joy and pride. They organized a party on the night of the graduation to show their support and offer some formal encouragement. As for the graduates, they relished their accomplishments and appreciated all, along the way, who made it possible. Most importantly, they just secured another reason to continue humming, "Le ça ira!" In fact, unbeknown to the future bride, Alex was already planning his engagement proposal party after he had accepted a well-paying job offer!

Alex shifted his focus toward securing his matrimonial future. Fully aware of Ai's exceptional qualities, he was determined to turn their engagement into an unforgettable occasion. He saw himself as nearing the ultimate prize in his somewhat traditional mindset. His plan unfolded against the backdrop of careful coordination, involving Ai's parents and some special guests, Chris, Ai's brother, and James, Alex's brother, flying in from L.A., California, under the guise of celebrating Ai's academic achievement. Unable to attend her graduation due to work commitments, Chris's arrival added an extra layer of surprise to Alex's meticulously crafted scheme. The chosen restaurant, a favorite of Ai's, was carefully selected with the help of Ai's mother, who enthusiastically supported her future son-in-law's "secret" endeavor.

Every detail had to be executed flawlessly to maintain the element of surprise, requiring everyone involved to keep the plan under wraps and behave as if nothing out of the ordinary was afoot. It was a collective effort, with families and close friends playing their part in orchestrating the perfect moment for Alex to express his love and commitment to Ai.

Three months had elapsed since their graduation, and finally, all the scrupulous planning Alex had undertaken seemed poised for execution. The private party room had been meticulously arranged and adorned, every detail tailored with the future bride, Ai, in mind. Tables designated for family members and close friends encircled the central focal point—the future couple's table—each seat carefully aligned with the seating chart prominently displayed at the entrance for guests' convenience.

As the anticipation built, the first arrivals were none other than their parents, eager to assist and liaise with the restaurant staff, ensuring the smooth orchestration of the evening's events. It was meticulously choreographed, with Alex slated to make his entrance after Ai and her brother Chris had settled at the designated table.

Curiosity sparked within Ai as she observed her brother's decision to join them in the party room rather than opt for a more intimate table in the main dining area. But any pondering was swiftly overtaken by the arrival of the guests and, to Ai's astonishment, Alex himself. With a signal imperceptible to most, the room filled with eager well-wishers, a tangible buzz of excitement enveloping the space.

A banner unfurled above their table, proudly proclaiming "Just Engaged," setting the stage for Alex's carefully orchestrated proposal. Against the melodic backdrop of "Dog Days Are Over" by Florence + The Machine, Jim stepped forward, ready to fulfill the expected ritual. Before Ai could offer her response, a chorus of jubilant "yeses" erupted from the assembled guests, led by Alex's exuberant family. Overwhelmed with emotion, Ai's eyes glistened with tears as she nodded in acceptance, her heart fluttering with joy and anticipation for the future ahead.

The remainder of the evening unfolded seamlessly, marked by delectable cuisine, flowing drinks, and lively conversations. As the engaged couple made their rounds to each table, expressing heartfelt gratitude, it was an opportunity for Ai to proudly display the newest symbol of her journey toward matrimony. Congratulations and well wishes abounded, with some daring souls venturing to inquire about the timing of the impending nuptials. With grace and warmth, Ai responded, "While we've yet to set an exact date tonight, I'm simply relieved that Alex has paved the way forward." Her words were met with understanding nods and warm smiles, affirming the joyous occasion and the promising future that lay ahead.

Chapter 10
Their Jumping in the Storm!

As many women can attest, wedding planning often begins long before a potential groom even considers proposing. For Ai, like countless others, envisioning every detail of her courtship and eventual marriage has been a cherished pastime since her teenage years. Now, with a real partner in mind, the challenge lies in ensuring his continued engagement and commitment until the momentous day arrives.

However, amidst the excitement, elements of wedding planning seem to remain firmly entrenched in the feminine domain. Will Ai's dreams for her special day resonate with her partner? Will Alex share her enthusiasm for selecting the perfect color palette, or will it be a trivial concern for him? Could he possibly understand the importance of choosing a picturesque location near the venue for memorable wedding photos? Will he ever contemplate the weather forecast for the big day, or will that detail be left entirely to chance?

And what about the finer details? Will he devote hours to finding the proper wedding attire or approach the task nonchalantly? Will the size and composition of the guest list weigh on his mind beyond mere financial considerations? As the planning progresses, will he demonstrate an interest in the logistics, such as the season and venue, or the selection of specific songs to accompany each significant moment of the celebration?

These questions linger as Ai navigates the intricate dance of wedding preparation, each one serving as a litmus test for her partner's commitment and understanding of her vision for their shared future. For in the culmination of their love story lies a union of hearts and a fusion of dreams, traditions, and aspirations that must find harmony on the day they say "I do."

"Why?" queried many a groom-to-be, their minds fixed on the significance of marriage beyond the ceremonial pomp. It's a curious divide; while women often perceive the wedding day and its accouterments as the zenith of their relationship, men adopt a more pragmatic, almost Machiavellian stance. For them, it's less about tangible milestones and more about the future dividends, albeit often imaginary, that await once they've played the role of the dutiful partner. Is there a panacea for this perennial dilemma?

One balmy Friday afternoon, nearly two years into his marriage with Ai, Alex pondered this question with a bemused expression on his face. He couldn't help but marvel at how willingly he'd embraced all the trappings of matrimony in pursuit of his then-paramour, now his beloved wife. Regret wasn't a sentiment he harbored; life had treated them well. Both Alex and Ai were gainfully employed, their schedules often mirroring each other's. Alex found fulfillment in managing a community housing project for the county, a role that came with a handsome salary and enviable benefits.

Meanwhile, a corporate lawyer, Ai, held the reins as the primary breadwinner. Their roles were clear, their dynamic harmonious. Hard work was their shared ethos, a necessity dictated by the demands of their respective professions.

Chapter 11
To The Calm Eye Of The Storm!

Ai and Alex's relationship had been sailing smoothly. Ai had diligently fulfilled her end of the bargain, ensuring Alex's culinary satisfaction in exchange for postponing their journey into parenthood. As a result, their bond flourished. They found themselves delving deeper into each other's worlds, providing unwavering support, and adapting to the evolving dynamics of their love. However, Ai wasn't content with just maintaining the status quo; she was determined to explore the realms of intimacy with her new man.

One sunny afternoon following their romantic honeymoon escapade, Ai presented her husband with a neatly wrapped package as they sifted through their wedding gifts. She unveiled her surprise with a mischievous glint in her eyes and a playful smirk. "Accepting this gift from me comes with a condition," she declared, her voice dripping with anticipation. "Henceforth, any request made by either of us is to be met with loving compliance, barring exceptional circumstances. And by 'exceptional,' I mean scenarios like me being stranded in Il Ciclo or you being struck by lightning—God forbid! Do we have a deal?" she teased, extending the gift to him with a sexually loaded smile.

Their laughter echoed through the room as Alex nodded in agreement, accepting the terms of Ai's proposition. Little did they know, this playful exchange would serve as a cornerstone for the intimacy and understanding that would continue to flourish in their relationship.

Their journey together was just beginning, filled with countless moments of joy, laughter, and unwavering love. As they navigated the complexities of married life, they would come to cherish these lighthearted moments, each strengthening their bond. Ai's playful spontaneity and Alex's unwavering commitment destined them for a lifetime of love and happiness.

In the vein of the adage, "all that glitters is not gold," the true essence and worth of gold can only be accurately assessed through stringent verification processes, like testing with fire. In a parallel narrative, the challenges of Alex's capabilities were keenly felt on the night of his wedding, thanks to his wife's intense expectations. Despite

Alex's prior claims regarding the vigor and resilience of his capabilities, he discovered his efforts were insufficient in meeting her robust and comprehensive demands during this critical juncture. Whereas he embarked on this endeavor with the zest typical of a short-distance runner, his partner was in search of the unwavering stamina characteristic of an ultramarathon competitor. Although there were brief instances of contentment, they were overshadowed by her ultimate dissatisfaction with his performance that evening. Reflecting upon the night, she observed, "Initially, there was a glimmer of hope, but it quickly faded. Still, his optimistic approach was commendable, and I made the best of what was offered. " The insightful wife summed up that pivotal night. When later asked about their intimate experience following a short vacation, she humorously remarked, "Think of it as the beginning of an extensive personal improvement program! I'm optimistic that my husband will eventually meet the expectations, especially since he's well aware that the market for both product and service is competitive."

Before Ai tied the knot, she delved into many narratives recounting shattered marriages shared by colleagues and friends. These stories echoed the betrayal of vows, where spouses dared to savor forbidden fruits or indulge in clandestine affairs. The question lingered: "Why...? Can this unsettling trend be averted?" For Ai, these queries transcended mere intellectual ponderings; they resonated with her on a deeply personal level. Like numerous others caught in the tumult of parental infidelity, Ai and her brother bore the scars not just from their childhood but also into their adulthood. She wasn't naive; she comprehended the allure of individuals deemed 'dangerously' captivating. In this era of indulgence, even committed partners might entertain desires for another, perhaps just for a fleeting moment, regardless of the time of day. Over time, Ai devised strategies to shield her future partner, not necessarily from entertaining such fantasies but from succumbing to the allure and having the means or inclination to act upon them. "Is such prevention feasible?" pondered Ai amidst the world's complexities.

Alex's anticipation reached a fever pitch as he carefully peeled back the layers of wrapping paper encasing his wife's thoughtful gift. Revealed before him was a title that promised intrigue: '365 sex Pos ....' "I love it!" he exclaimed before even fully absorbing the contents, his enthusiasm mirroring that of a child catching sight of the ice cream truck on a scorching summer afternoon. Gratitude overwhelmed him as he turned to his wife, enveloping her in a tender embrace followed by a sweet kiss.

"Thank you, my love," he murmured, his heart brimming with appreciation. "I had a feeling you'd appreciate it," she responded with a knowing smile. "It's all part of my strategy to help alleviate, if not eradicate, your AVD organically. But I want us to embark on this journey together as a family. Your feedback will be invaluable, as always."

Beneath the surface of Ai's seemingly simple gift lay a meticulously crafted plan composed of three distinct prongs: *Strategic "Desecration," Strategic Demystification,* and *Strategic Shell*. It was akin to a mother sending her spirited adolescent son off to a boot camp, albeit within the safe confines of their home. The objective? To channel Alex's energy into constructive endeavors while safeguarding the sanctity of their marriage.

Ai couldn't fathom the idea of her husband straying beyond the bounds of their union. Thus, instead of shipping her energetic man off to a remote training facility, she resolved to cultivate a "special matrimonial environment" where they could both thrive. The impetus behind her project stemmed from a genuine desire to fortify their bond, which was grounded in trust and mutual respect.

This narrative, rooted in truth, serves as a poignant reminder of Ai's unwavering commitment to her partner and their shared future.

Chapter 12
Where The Sahel And Sahara Dust Meet the Tropical Clouds

Culture has its own time and space. There you will find the usuals and the unexpected. The beauty and the ugly. The licit and the forbidden. The verbal and the non-verbal communications. Certain things are exposed and others are hidden ones. Certain rules are well spelled out in the book but many are rather branded on the community's heart and conscience. They are indelible. There also, you will find a vast generational knowledge bank with a river of layered ignorance that has been running alongside it. However, sometimes they criss-crossed peacefully but other times violent clashes did take place when one was getting too close for the other one's comfort. Such encroachment would not be tolerable, especially by the latter! Moreover, within such time and space, all people are marching in, even the flora and the fauna aren't beyond its long, powerful arm.Therein, people's aspirations and their inherited precious lethargy are well cherished. Still in there, the lush, grassy land and the parched fields perpetually coexist. Search and you'll find both the official and the informal. And also, the sacred and the profane are inherent parts of it. And, like on treacherous terrain, be careful where you set your foot on! For you may cause an abrupt, absurd avalanche of nonsense or, worse, you may find yourself on unsettling quick sand at your own risk, despite its rock solid appearance!

To capture its ever elusive sense, here is a story of a couple visiting a foreign country as tourists. It was Winter time. So, like migrating birds, Stephie and Marty went South, searching for the Sun. Who wouldn't? Most people would prefer soaking in such precious heat along a beautiful beach. Stephie is always down for that while Marty's preference was for anything green. However, since another great word for marriage is compromise, the lovely couple had a merry time together: one day they were on the beach and the other in the botanical garden. Partners in such relationships, where logic and mutual consideration prevail, tend to last longer and be happier. They found themselves "blended" well with the locals while enjoying all of what the area had to offer. However, soon they will find out that dancing like the locals requires much more than just learning the new moves of the dance du jour!

During this lazy Sunday, Stephie and Marty opted to visit an orchard with exotic hors d'œuvre and wine testing on the menu. Taking a leisurely walk in there and breathing in its intriguing scents in such an enchanting environment was just therapeutic, they conceded. "Wouldn't it be good if we could do such activities more often when we return back home!," she wondered. Marty shook his head in agreement and then smiled. The morning sun dappled through the leaves of the olive trees, casting a cool, green light on Stephie and Marty as they wandered deeper into the orchard. The air was thick with the heady perfume of ripe olives, a scent that brought a sense of unusual calm to her. They were at a beautiful orchard located in a small village nestled in between Africa and the Caribbean Sea, far from the daily commotion of their usually busy city life.

The enchanted couple got the shock of their life. They saw a couple in their sixties charging towards Vechio in their direction. They were Vecchio and his wife Ladona, as they later learned their names. Vecchio, clearly pissed off, just hit Marty's stretched out right hand down as he was pointing out at some nearby blossoming trees to draw his wife's attention there! She cannot help herself but to ask the obvious but absurd question: "Why?" For they both knew that they didn't do "nothing" deserving such a strong reaction from the gentleman. But obviously, in this particular situation, what the couple thought was irrelevant, has apparently a paramount meaning otherwise what just happened wouldn't happen, right? So they were eagerly waiting for a sensible explanation from the still angry man.

"You can't do that!," a still annoyed Vechio shouted.

The foreigners were also more confused! "Sir, we're deeply sorry for making you upset. We didn't mean it. But, can you please tell us now what we did to make you so irritated?," a contrite Marty inquired on behalf of them both.

"By pointing at them, you will hinder the flowering trees from producing sufficient fruits! How would we be able to take care of my family then?," said Vechio, as an The explanation to the motives behind his behavior, this time a bit less pissed.

This indigenous explanation plunged the couple into further confusion!

"How in the world is this even possible? Who vested me with such awesome power and since when?," wondered Marty completely flabbergasted.

Then, it was Vecchio's turn to be shocked in disbelief that this forty-something couple in front of him doesn't know this basic fact about the proper timing to point at growing fruit trees. That and other similar stories that have been told time and again for ages by grand-parents and the likes in the community. Remember what is "Absurd can be true at the same time!" for, at the end, it always depends on the beholder's perspective or mindset.

"So you weren't from here, are you! I had a knee-jerk reaction when I saw you standing there. You look like the other fellow who cunningly tried to ruin my harvest last year. Because of him, we lost a quarter of it! So we barely made it through last Winter. Mam, do you understand where I am coming from?," he directly asked Stephie, seeing that he wasn't going anywhere with Marty in any shape and form.

"Sir, are you trying to make us believe that, by pointing at some of your olive trees, somehow it would negatively impact your yields? Sir, the science behind plant growth has absolutely nothing to do with anything that you've been saying! Scientific studies and methodologies in the past decades have done away with such empirical anecdotal theories and mindset. And you hit my husband for what again? Really! You should apologize to us!," she demanded him with a serious face, his persistence with such fallacy clearly got under her skin.

Half hour or so of back and forth both parties remained more entrenched in their understanding and positions. "Timari pap monte e Timari pap desann." The locals' minds are well locked up in folkloric credos. Forgetting that no one conversation will ever be enough to alter an old man's mindset, Marty made a last ditch effort to help Vecchio to at least consider that maybe his views on the matter might not be 100% exact. "Why don't you check out "plant growth" on Google?," he suggested.

"What for? I have been farming all my life. So did my grand-parents and their grand-parents! Enough of your heartlessness and your insults! Get out of here!, otherwise we'll escort you out!," a dyspeptic Vecchio finally lashed out.

And they did, fast! Later, at their hotel, Stephie and Marty still couldn't wrap up their minds around the surreal experience they just had with Mr. Vecchio. "So we still have folks like him around in this day and age, don't we? What can make people so obscurantist and obstinate? Have they been on some kind of traditional medicine since infancy? Could such an attitude be innate or is it gradually acquired as a hallmark of some people of certain parts of the country or certain parts of the world?," A disturbed Stephie kept asking both her husband who was standing in front of the small bathroom mirror and, in fact, to herself, too.

The lady's century-old questions definitely fit in this Time and Space but definite answers are well beyond at the same time and space! No wonder the man in the mirror, upon hearing them, has raised both hands up in the air signaling acceptance of the fact he is powerless before such an overwhelming amount of obstinate stupidity. Then, in hindsight, they both questioned the wisdom behind their attempt to reason with Vecchio and Ladona. Apparently, they mistakenly equated his soft demeanor with a soft heart and mind! Finally, his wife was about to ask Marty what it will take for such people to change the they are but then she remembered this Hebrew proverb that states:

"Even if you pound a fool with a pestle

Like crushed grain in a mortar,

His foolishness will not leave him."

Culture to their rescue! Having that in mind then has helped Marty and Stephie to look at Vecchio's intransigence from another perspective. They realized that Vecchio and the likes will likely remain the way they are. Therefore, no need to let Vecchio's obstination and obscurantism mess up their day any further. Also, no need to keep twisting the body and mind in an attempt to pierce through such impenetrable ignorance. Marty appreciated his wife's insight very much. So he canceled his plan to get a coup de clairin to calm his nerves and mind before going to bed that night. They slept well that night after so much physical and mental exercises earlier at Vecchio's place.

Stephie and Marty's vacation in the region took an unexpected expected turn. But they focus on the big picture. For, make no mistake, they still love the people, the place, the landscape, the cuisine, the beautiful beaches on the shorelines but they, as some regular "visitors" before them, came to grip with The Fact that the majority of the local people's minds have been set by type M mortar! Would you dare what countless visitors like Stephie and Marty did? I bet that you won't if you are aware that we all live within time and space!

As we learned earlier, cyclically the Sahel and Sahara dust mixes with the tropical clouds. This phenomenon is at the basis of many relations, such as the Singleton's. They met at a social gathering at one of Rachel's friends almost two decades ago. Mr. Pyram and Rachel Singleton have been together for almost seventeen years but have been married for 14 of them. Their union is the typical occurrence when the Sahel and the Sahara dust and the tropical clouds meet up. They atypically delayed matrimony and parenthood to focus on their schooling and their professional career. However, in that area the biological clock is real. It's the measuring reed of womanhood and manhood. Also, few can escape the long, powerful arm of cultural pressure, regardless of current geographical coordinates. Nonetheless to say that the couple have two children Sebby 13 years old and Emma 11. Along with Rachel's parents living there, the couple deliberately created a lively environment for their kids to thrive. Really, they made it easy to talk about anything. But there are certainly things that family won't talk about.

Do you have your own children? Have you ever observed the way they ask questions? Curiosity is the fuel that keeps a child's young mind going. They are typically very inquisitive about everything and want to understand their surrounding environment. The Singleton's aren't the exception. At around 3 years old, Sebby and Emma started to ask their parents questions about things they absolutely rather not talk about. They are relentless, though. Many start asking as soon as they learn to speak. With wide, eager eyes, they look up at you and ask such things as: Why are the trees green? What are they made of? Who taught the animal to run? It looks like they have another "Why?" ready, even after your best answers! For some parents, such moments provide them with an opportunity to support their child's learning and to build thinking ability. For others, they are just nightmares!

If you are a parent, do you cherish yours? If you were, what kind of parent do you think you would be? What about if you stop reading to ask your teen, would she/he say that you're comfortable to talk about their sexuality questions in a calm and dignified way? Your answer will likely depend to a large extent on the time and space you were born and raised. It doesn't mean you will be condemned one way or the other. It simply means that it may require on your part more or less effort in order to welcome your child's questions rather than dread them. Sometimes it's a timing issue. Parents are busier than ever in the hustle and bustle of modern life. However, mostly it's a content issue for folks who symbolically and culturally live around the Caribbean Sea and Africa inclusively. The younger Singleton's belong to the latter group. The senior Singleton's have always been part of it as for the rest of the family and for most parents in many other parts of the world. What's the toughest sexuality question a child ever asked you? What was your initial reaction? And why?

The www.thetalkinstitute.com website gives a list of some of the toughest questions kids asked. Here is a sample: "What is sex?" "Were you a virgin when you got married?" " Where do babies come from?" "What age is right for sex?" "What is porn?" (February 01, 2017).

"S.e.x Talking about that…topic has always been our family's "Shibboleth!," confessed Rachel. What does she mean by that? The word shibboleth is based on the biblical account regarding two Israelite tribes, the Ephraimites and the Gileadites, each pronounced the word "shibboleth" and "sibboleth" respectively due regional accent. After a terrible war between them, when a fugitive from Ephraim tried to go back home, the Gileadites who captured the Jordan River fords leading to Ephraim asked them to pronounce shibboleth as a kind of linguistic password that would verify which ethnic group they belong to. Since the Ephraimites' pronunciation "*sibboleth*" was different from their own pronunciation, the person in question was instantly seized and killed. "We dread the topic of sexuality because in our culture we equate talking with doing it, encouraging it and flaming wrong desires! Also, we are afraid of saying the wrong thing or the wrong way in front of our kids, family or others. Like in the case of the poor Ephraimites, the best thing for everyone is for our kids or anybody else not to ask that kind of question. It's our family motto "Don't ask, Don't tell," as regards to sexuality. "Please don't misinterpret that! The old houses will continue to rumble and thunder! There should be no question about that. Folks like us will answer no question about "it,"" stated Rachel with big laughs!

"As far back as I can remember, as a child, I never heard our grand-parents, parents utter The word or any other similar words directly related to "it". It's just taboo. S.e.x is not a word that you would hear under any Singleton's roof, until today! It's weird because I am in my forties and we're from large families. So we love making "babies". The Singleton's do but won't say!," Rachel finally continued as the spokesperson for so many people here and beyond. Rachel remembered clearly how livid she was one day after school Sebby and Emma teamed up to ask her: "At what age should people have s.e.x?" She was so terrified she almost faithed. And so close to literally hitting him in the mouth! That's one of the reasons such families invented some sort of elaborated hybrid language system where euphemism is heavily used for any word or expression that can convey any hint of sexuality. Is this the best approach? Or is there a better, sensible way for responsible parents to address sexuality questions with their curious kids?

Failure to find and adopt such a reasonable approach can cause unattended consequences ranging from the absurd to the tragic. One day, the cleaning lady inadvertently dropped the Singleton's "do book" somewhere under their master bedroom bed. No big deal. Life goes on in the Singleton's household. One weekend, Rachel wanted to check out the "menu" because she had "a taste" for something "exotic dish". Her husband reached out for the "book" to check out "the ingredients and the instructions" but his hand came back to him empty. Where is the "book?" He didn't dare asking Rachel a second question after seeing the look on her face! So Pyram went to ask Singleton Senior discreetly. He didn't have it. Sebby was next in line. "Which book is it, dad?" He gave him a vague color description! "I am not sure that I saw such a book around. Sorry! "Are you sure, Seb?," his dad asked in a hushed voice. "Yeah! What is its title or what is it about?" A clearly frustrated Pyram turned his back without bothering to answer further. He frantically continued his searching with no success that day! Sometimes, they make themselves helpless and ridiculous by their sheer hypocrisy!

Other times, it's their kids who never learned the healthy way and paid a tragic price. Like the following report shows. In a secondary school in Nigeria, a sexually promiscuous girl used to advise her fellow students about sex. They listened to her eagerly, even though her ideas were full of nonsense that she had gleaned from pornographic literature. Some of the girls experimented with her advice. As a result, one girl got pregnant out of wedlock and died of a self-induced abortion. How terrible! To avoid primrose paths for ourselves, for our loved ones, may we all continue to invest time and effort to choose a road with a known destination, not necessarily the one that our culture, folklore, geography or the majority dictate. Indeed, certain things are beyond our control because we live within time and space. However, when it comes to our relationship with our partners, remember that we live as if we'll sleep in the bed we have made ourselves.

Chapter 13
When "Harry" failed to meet "Sally"

Harry Madden, now in his mid-twenties, grew up in the same neighborhood as Sally, who was 23 years old then. They went to the same high school. They even frequented the same neighborhood church. So they usually saw each other quite often every week for quite some time. They frequented the same circle of friends. Some of Harry's friends knew he always had a crush on Sally. Although she was aware of it, in her teen years, she considered him a brother, never a potential marital partner.

One Saturday night, at a social gathering, Harry, seeing Sally talking with her friends as if for the first time, was drawn to her in a male way. She also noticed something new in how he looked at her. So, during an opportune time, on her way to use the lady's room that night, Harry had finally managed to ask Sally out to get to know her better, he said. Sally was not in any romantic relationship then and always thought Harry was cute and friendly. Although she was amused by his "unexpected request, she felt that she needed to run the idea of her dating Harry to Michelle, one of her best friends, and the other girls before giving a firm yes. It turned out that everybody loved Harry! So Sally went to church that Sunday, not to remotely hear the Gospel, but to tell Harry her own good news!

In general, religious folks don't entangle themselves in hot, romantic relationships unless they are in forbidden ones. For duty, temptations and physiological worries tend to cocoon them until the heavens bestow formal blessings over their union. So, Sally and Harry, like a couple preparing for their third marriage in their fifties, did not have time on their side. Harry and Sally's first date went well. It was in a "safe" restaurant where the environment was conducive to serious conversations in a free atmosphere. They have known each other for a long time. Nothing disturbing in their past. Both were working. They need to be married first... Harry wanted three children, but Sally only wanted two. However, both finally agreed to leave any firm numbers in the Lord's good hands. No significant changes were expected logistically besides the fact that they would be under the same roof after their wedlock. They talked about chaperoning arrangements in the future. Harry and Sally planned to inform their religious elders of their wedding timetable very soon.

About seven months later, Harry duly married Sally. No bedding ceremony took place; they weren't British after all! But something genuinely epic took place that nuptial night. Instead, it was what didn't happen when Sally met with Harry and especially why the marriage was not consummated that caused Ai to see the necessity for couples to at once demystify it as soon as possible, but progressively, if need be, respecting each other's sensibility. People tend to resist even changes that would benefit them because they are too comfortable within their own societal or cultural cocoon, even within their ignorance. "Alex and I want to be a different kind of couple," said Ai as she learned more about Harry's nuptial night saga.

The wedded couple arrived at their honeymoon vacation hotel. Raw, animalistic lust radiated from their minds and bodies and filled up the entire room. No pickup lines were needed. So Harry rushed to get "ready" in the bathroom while Sally, standing by her nuptial bed, prepared herself, not much for what was coming, but rather for how it would manifest itself! Moments later, Harry emerged from there, his "sword" drawn, and, with the determination of a lion, approached his prey for their first intimate dance. Upon seeing the approaching anatomic spectacle, Sally screamed from the top of her voice and, caught up in the whys and the wherefores, forbade him from getting any closer to her! Utterly confused, Harry wondered what could be wrong with his brand-new wife. Wasn't it what she signed up for in getting married? As for Sally, traumatized and still in shock by the mechanism of couple intimacy, bewildered by her "new" Harry! Both were distracted by their own ignorance. And unfortunately, regardless of its causes, distraction tends to kill passion. So when Harry and Sally finally calmed down and resigned from the situation, they agreed to try doing it tomorrow. But during what could have been their wedding night loaded with hot, smoking passion, Sally slept soundly in her denim, to Harry's consternation!

In the morning, the newlyweds had their breakfast in bed. Harry had selected his meal, mindful of what was next in their schedule. Afterward, Harry was more than ready to meet up with Sally to make up for the initial failed test drive. However, during his second attempt, an anxious Sally, second-guessing Chouchoune's ability to host her husband's flesh work fittingly, fell awkwardly off the bed! As a result,

Sally hurt her back and her left foot. Then, she was technically not in the mood for the remainder of their honeymoon stay! "Ah! The right mind! How vital is it for intimacy? But, for a lasting marriage, Long live compartmentalization!" said Harry in his frustrated mind. So not only was she out of commission during the remainder of her honeymoon, but she also had to go through physical therapy for months when they finally returned back home. And, much later, got back at "it!"

What a frustrating honeymoon they both had, indeed! Harry and Sally had waited for that moment for years to see it needlessly wasted! For they were duly entitled to physical intimacy; in fact, they both dreamt about it and wanted it badly all along, but anatomical and physiological confusions denied them its timely enjoyment. How vexing! "Expectation postponed makes the heart sick," said an old Hebrew proverb. How sadly true for Harry and Sally!

"Unbelievable!" said Alex after hearing the new couple's nightmarish story.

"But, his wife quickly added, unfortunately, it's true! I am wondering if poor Harry and Sally would ever recover from such mishaps!"

So, to promote knowledge and dispel misconceptions within their walls, the younger Phillips create different games or activities that provide ample 'training' and pleasures for all involved.

Chapter 14
Enjoying The Calm Eye Of The Storm

Harry and Sally's true story made Ai ever more determined to create an all-encompassing environment so as to properly enjoy her life with her husband. "Use what you got to get what you want," Ai kept reminding herself.

Erogenous Mapping "Project" (EMP):

Ai remembered how mystified one of her guy friends was during a figure drawing class in college. The naked model came in and sat down with all the excited male students around her. "No metal feathers were strong enough to contain ourselves, and no air conditioning system could have been strong enough to cool us down during the drawing sessions. Our imagination just went wild because her body's radiating impact on us was real!" her friend used to tell her. If anything, her experience with Alex has taught her that passing the time alone was not enough to make even a married man familiar with another feminine body.

"Love, would you have time to help me with a family project tomorrow afternoon?" Ai candidly asked her husband after she finished opening and sorting out more wedding gifts that Friday afternoon.

"Sure! I will be happy to. Will we need any specific tools or things of that nature?" an enthusiastic Alex replied.

She smiled and answered: "Thanks, babe. We already have all we need. Just get our couple of notebooks and a working pen or pencil ready. OK?" she concluded.

Alex liked everything he heard about that project, especially its mysterious but alluring title: "Pleasure Spots Mapping Project."

That night, Alex thought about his wife's undefined project so much so that he dreamt that she had asked him to soap up her back while she was taking a shower in the middle of Time Square …

When Saturday came, they had an early dinner. Ai fed her husband baked salmon with baby kale and spinach. She had a bottle of green apple moscato and didn't allow him to have more than half a glass of red wine. Needless to say, Alex helped out his wife with the dishes, unprompted, mind you, because, knowing his wife, like some other women, if there were dirty dishes in the kitchen sink, that could sink his chances that she would later properly express her gratitude ...

"Thanks, honey, for helping out. I will be waiting for you downstairs. Please don't forget to come down with our note-taking materials," his wife said as she headed to the basement, where a furnished bedroom awaited.

"Welcome! Ai said to her husband as he was entering the bedroom. "Love, everything under this bathrobe is legally yours. So naturally, I want you to be familiarized with what's yours while you will be helping me know where to put each spot or section on my pleasure scale. I hope that during another session, we will reverse the roles. Do you have any problem with our project's scope so far, my love?

"'Problem?' I am freaking loving it!" she heard him saying. His wife's laughter surprised him because he didn't mean to verbalize his excitement.

"It's OK. I am glad that you do. But tonight, I would be some kind of executive director, directing you as to where, when, how, at what speed, and the appropriate pressure level to probe my body out, even the soft parts, and then l let you know how l topically feel as you would stop intermittently to write down some succinct notes, if at all possible. Can you handle that, my love? Let's begin. Shall we?" she said, letting her bathrobe fall smoothly to the floor.

Suddenly, Alex beheld the most environmentally friendly two-piece suit ever seen on a woman: his wife's doped-up, popped-up body was barely covered by the top of her two-piece suit, and the rest of it was basically a complex and attractive meshy medley!

At that precise moment, Alex realized that playing his part in the project would be his life's most challenging job!

He had barely recovered from what he was hearing and then seeing that his wife added:

"I dressed as insubstantially as humanly possible to avoid unduly restricting your work areas. However, you have a standing authorization to remove or rip them off at any moment you deem it necessary or just because you feel like it. You may start at my dorsal, from the top down to my feet. When you're done, you will continue ventrally. Then you will receive specific instructions about how to proceed when you get to the vag area. But, sweetheart, remember, I am your wife; it's always OK to share your feelings and desires with me, regardless of their nature. I don't want to torture you unduly or anything. So please know that I can cool you off anytime and then continue this session later, OK?" she sympathetically instructed him as she was lying down on the bed.

Alex intermittently stopped to succinctly write down his wife's sensual feedback along with part or section of his body and the kind of manipulation that generated such responses. But the only thing that he heard from all his wife just said was, as his request, 'she would be willing to put an end to his agony!' After hearing the good news, he resolved to hold fast as long as possible before uttering the SOS signal to his "capable and willing" wife. Alex wanted to take it as a personal endurance challenge. Also, as a token of his wife's generosity, he wanted to selflessly allow her to get as much pleasure as she had been giving him since they'd been married.

Alex tried to cover as many body areas as humanly possible downstairs before asking for his wife's help, meticulously mapping his belle's erogenous areas of her body. By then, all his manly impulses had put his body and soul under tremendous pressure! He sensed that his masculine resistance was finally at its inflection point! He felt that his whole self suddenly geared up in survival mode! In a knee-jerk reaction, he ripped off his wife's two-piece stringy and threw what was left of it to the floor! Poor him! Visibly, he had reached his limit! Fortunately for him, she noticed it; she sensed that her husband's hands, his abnormal breathing, and his entire body were as hot as the center of the Sun! As a result of Alex's ongoing mapping work, Ai herself has been feeling like a tropical forest deep inside. "Enough! I will take some mental notes to complete our erogenous mapping and then add them up to yours later," she said with a mild voice but inhuman tone. So, to prevent her husband from collapsing from heat exhaustion and, for her own sake too, she was ready to let her husband start up the cooling session, at last! What a relief for all!

To cool things off, all parties mutually were agreeable to the sequence, as they were interchangeably taking the lead this time in the escalating to de-escalate process. That unusual strategy seemed to be working! Indeed, he got good priming traction and great feedback for his expert maneuvers with both being averse to location discrimination. And, remember, Ai and Alex have ever been like Sunday drivers!

After they emptied their life out, Alex said to his then-subcooled wife: "Thank you for everything!"

"No worries!" she replied with a relaxed tone; I like what you did for me and to me this afternoon. The "worker" deserves his wages, right? You wouldn't complain in case I find creative ways to keep you busy around the house, which is such a mundane activity, would you? Or was this session helpful to you at all?"

After hearing his wife, Alex, though unarmed, jumped on her to kiss and to express his love for her, for her, for her attractive mind, her attitude, and, above all, her strategic douceur in dealing with him, a man after all.

"It's a resounding "no" to your first question. That's what I signed for. I dreamed of such opportunities all my life; it's really my dream job!" And I thoroughly enjoyed our mapping exercises. I feel that I am getting more and more familiar with your "terrain." But how would I remember my way around there since the "landscape" is so fascinating and mind-blowing?" an excited Alex said.

"Fantastic! Don't worry! Be happy because we're going to have many more similar sessions. I want you to be my "landscaper for life!"

"Amen to that! We need some cold drinks!"

Alex said as he went upstairs to fetch some.

When he returned, he found his wife lying in the same attire Eve had worn before the Fall. He brought up a glass of Moscato and some snacks but lost them again in her shape and form; he almost dropped the snack off the floor instead of in his wife's extended hand!

"Thanks, love! Like you had read my mind! Do you want to watch something, or would you like to keep gazing at my body for the remainder of the night?" Ai jokingly asked her still-mesmerized husband.

Alex ended up doing both that night.

They regularly had such 'learning' sessions with his wife, frequently in the lead. She tried to kill off several birds during the Deconsecration phase of the multi-phase program. First, such sessions helped Alex develop enough knowledge of her anatomy to be strategically comfortable around her body and soul. Secondly, they had allowed him to develop a coroner's sang-froid whenever the time came to carve her elephant up. Finally, taking advantage of those showdowns will prevent her poor husband from repeatedly falling into the cheetah's trap. Those big cats run very fast to catch their prey. But they become so exhausted afterward that they become vulnerable to other predators that either attack them or eat up their hard-earned lunch during their recovery period. Then, their strength has become their weakness. "It's not so tragic when another predator eats an unattended fresh kill. However, It's a tragedy whenever an opportunist beast of prey feasts on it because the former unnecessarily stumbled!" Ai used to tell her about Alex, her husband. Therefore, he was responsible for making the best of his wife's private exercises to heed her implied warning because forewarning is to be forearmed. Isn't it?

Mental Demystification

"Ay! The Sandbergs! See how fresh and lush Lily is over there! Oh my..! How many times have I felt an urge to trek on her way?

Oh! How well my mind knows the path!

For there are no spots, dead patches, or thinning sections.

No doubt Gary keeps her well-watered, mowing her properly and doing it to a T for his lady wife to look so dazzling!

"Oh yeah! Did he do a great job keeping others off of his lawn? Moreover, no one ever sees any weeds over there!

"Gary must be an expert in using natural fertilizer and must have found the right turf, the kind I have been looking for …

"Therefore, what not to give to 'care for.. or take a stroll ' in Gary's park, even for just a ratio!" lamented Thom, Sandberg's envious neighbor.

For a while, that has been Thom's burning desire, the result of how he pictured Lily Sandberg's grassy pasture! Like countless other men before him, Thom was clearly on his way head down toward "the other woman's trap."

Thom's perception mirrored that of Sam Dawson's, the man with the IQ of a seven-year-old child, who complained to Rita Harrison, a successful lawyer with a picture-perfect husband in the movie "I am Sam": "You don't know what it's like when you try, and you try, and you try, and you try, and you don't ever get there! You're perfect because you were born perfect, and I was born like this!"

"You think you've got the market cornered on human suffering? Let me tell you something about people like me. People like me feel lost, and little, and ugly, and dispensable. People like me have husbands, screwing other people far more perfect than me. People like me have sons who hate them!" she then replied, visibly frustrated.

Did Sam get the point? Would the Thoms out there ever accept that even the most beautiful woman in the world would never be able to give more than she has?

How many men do you know who, single or married, have longed for, pursued, and ultimately fell into "the perfection plus trap?" Why do they "desire another woman's beauty in their hearts Or allow her to captivate them with her alluring eyes or curves?"

"One could understand why folks who have limitations similar to Dawson's could be so mistaken, but why have countless intelligent, successful men committed adultery?" Ai wondered. She was never able to wrap her head around it. However, then married, the second phase of her program regimen aims to give Alex one less reason to follow Rita's husband's path, not even mentally, she hopes. "Will it ever work?" Cindy once asked her. "That's exactly the purpose of the next phase of our couple activities," she pointedly answered.

"Many men, even those having plenty of access to women, seem to have serious difficulty remembering what a female is whenever they see a thin, pretty woman with generous bazookas nearby. They often reacted as if they just discovered a new creature among humankind! So, at least, mentally, they would try to identify its anatomic makeup and even explore the whole thing by graciously and methodically removing all her "*coquetterie de l'occident!*" Apparently, such men often fail to realize that dazzling beauty is just another woman, just like the one they have at home or next to them sometimes! Consequently, they want to pursue her, to create opportunities for further or real "exploration," without considering the multidimensional consequences!" Ai grappled with the question of why another woman's body could still mystify a boyfriend or husband. What could a wife do to prevent her man from going down that primrose path? Is there an antidote for that? Yes, what could I do to keep my husband in line? Would he ever accept to "re-wire up his mind?"

Simulate to Debunk

"The day we stop looking would be the day we die!" Alex replied after his wife later shared her thoughts and potential concerns mentioned in the above section.

"True!" She conceded. " But, what do you think, honey? Is it really true that there is no harm in looking as I have heard so many guys proclaim?" his wife continued, trying to poke his mind further on the matter.

"As a man, I tend to believe that looking is harmless. I am interested in hearing your thoughts since you insisted on having mine. Love, have I done something that bothered you in that regard?" Asked Alex anxiously.

"Oh! Not at all! If that was the case, you know I wouldn't be beating around the bush to bring it up to you. As I mentioned earlier, it seems there is a perennial risk for an initial quick look to turn later into something that would be detrimental to one's family. I don't want that to ever happen to us. Since "prevention is better than cure," I have been thinking about what we can do further to avoid falling into the "just looking trap." That's all," Ai finally said matter-of-factly.

"Ah! I see! What else could you do besides what we have been…? As intelligent agents, shouldn't we be able to take control of ourselves and stop mindlessly following our "other bellies" whenever our eyes rest on some passerby Bellissima? Or should practical wives blindfold their men and become their only authorized guides whenever they have to venture outside of the safe environment of their houses? Unless they just put them in chains at home so no potential temptresses would ever be in sight!" proposed Alex jokingly, but open to see if his ever-creative wife had better ideas.

Indeed, she did! On her way back to the dining room after deserving the table, a satisfied Ai came and then sat on her husband, facing him. So instantly, the dining area's temperature got hotter and conductively caused other "things" to get hot, and, for a good reason, with a good infrared device, one could see condensation already dripping off their ceiling as a result! In fact, from the top of the chair to the kitchen floor, not a single ounce of energy was lost. The "work" they have done together perfectly illustrates the law of energy conservation! The couple was satisfied with the "itinerary taken" and the "climactic end."

"What other occasions could you be fully satisfied in this life just after emptying your soul? A pensive Alex rhetorically asked in the aftermath.

"Love, thanks for your cooperation! How were we?" an ever-relaxed Ai asked her, then content man amusingly.

"Love, you surely can depend on my standing collaboration anytime! Such an attitude would keep any reasonable man well-fed and possibly away from falling into "the perfection plus trap," replied Alex.

"Marriages don't break up on account of infidelity. It's just a symptom that something else is wrong," stated Ai to change gears. "I just don't want to be the source of it nor want to behave like a capitalist wife by artificially creating and managing scarcity for symbolic gains. Moreover, I prefer that we have a generous system where my man always gets more for less, hoping that the cumulative or scalable benefits would be long-lasting!" she explained. "What say you, chérie?"

"Amen to all you just said, If what I heard is actually what you meant!" Alex excitedly replied.

"Then we're on the same page, baby! Wives need to find ways to imprint on their husbands' minds the bare but the whole truth about the opposite sex," continued his wife.

"You got me interested! What is it, love?" He curiously wondered.

"The fact is that "even the most beautiful woman in the whole world wouldn't be able to give a man more than she has." She explained.

Alex, making sure that he got the point, quickly asked: "Does it mean that, even though one couldn't see everything, they already know everything out there?"

"Basically, yes! All things considered!" His wife frankly answered.

"I know that you're correct, sweetie! But why is it so darn hard for many of us to act on that knowledge in sight of a curvy beauty?" Alex honestly asked.

"It's due mainly to men's incomprehensible forgetfulness and their wild, supercharged imagination!" she bluntly replied.

"But are we helpless, love?" her husband desperately wanted to know.

"Not at all! With proper "training," one could learn how, at the end of the day, to bring his feral imagination home with known reality, right? So love, don't worry! I have a few things to try out to help you thoroughly enjoy your wife with no excess capacity. We can start tomorrow after work. Are you interested!" suggested his wife.

On hearing it, Alex's imagination went wild! That night, he looked at his calendar on his phone, and he feels getting "trained" by his lady overrides all else. Thus, he decided to clear it up. He even had several adult dreams that night. Moreover, Throughout that workday, he could barely concentrate! His body was not indifferent about what he foresaw happening at home after work! So his jacket and his tight Tommy John were his best allies. Therefore, he kept the former on all day long to avoid potentially awkward situations!

In the morning, his wife, for her part, had all the after-work part of the day figured out. First of all, she dressed up not just for work but also for her afternoon" in-house sessions" with her husband in mind. Outwardly, she looked as professional as a corporate lawyer could be but also seemed as beautiful and sexy as an escort girl beneath the deceptive surface. Indeed, underneath that professional appearance, Ai wore a micro thong string breakaway adjustable at very low risk for "training" purposes. Certainly, she felt bare! Finally, she planned to be home *before* her husband so she would have enough time to set things up for another routine. The young couple, nonetheless, would be an epic night for any average family.

"Distraction kills time." Both Alex and Ai could testify to its veracity that day. Their focus was hardly on what they were doing at work. For example, his mind mainly wandered to possible contours of what came next after that while his wife had found herself titillating all day from all her feminine secrets du jour.

"Home, sweet home!" Alex kept humming on his commute home that afternoon. Which man wouldn't? However, with a more flexible schedule, his wife got there first, as her plans called for it. Then, she set up a bar tool with her husband's name on it, providing him a panoramic view of the dining and living rooms. She texted him about the seating arrangement and enamored him to respect it for his own benefit, which she said gave an extra motivation boost. So, the countdown for her husband's private show has begun!

Alex did as instructed when he finally made it home, like an old, obedient schoolboy. Waiting for the pleasure bait, even though he did not yet know in which form it would appear this time … After a few moments that lasted too long, he could hear his wife's steps approaching in his direction. Suddenly, she appeared, standing in front of him in all her symmetric curves but still dressed up as she left for work that morning. He tried as hard as possible to hide his disappointment, not knowing how utterly deceptive her professional appearance was. Unbeknown to him, there was quite less covering by design than it first appeared!

As she went back and forth between their living room and the dining room, Alex, then seeing the invisible and already enjoying it … in his male imagination, became troubled in his very core. As previously agreed, he had to write everything down in the couple's notebook. He realized that putting such thoughts, desires, and fantasies in written form was more complex than he thought. So, as his male frustration built up, his task became virtually impossible. Fortunately, his lady knew his limit, so she was sympathetic to her husband's plight. Thus, she attempted to provide him with some respite by giving him a "promotion!"

Alex's new assignment consisted of removing any clothes that her workplace's decency dictated. He excitedly complied! What a scene! Her undergarments were so insubstantial that they could be best described as a physical reveal, a let-it-all-hang-out, for his sheer satisfaction. However, Ai asked him to take new notes as she continued to wander back and forth like a model during a fashion show, his private show! A living but private carnival, indeed! After a while, he felt overwhelmed by all kinds of male desires. Of course, not all of them were human, Alx later confessed.

After a long time, almost ten thousand years in the man's mind, his wife instructed him to follow into the upstairs primary bathroom. Just imagine the scene as she began to deambulate in the direction of the stairs. With each step up she took in front of him, he saw all the colors in the world! He wanted to "finish her up" right then and there the very moment that he saw her downstairs earlier! But he knew that he needed to march on because, during one day each week, either he or Ai is scheduled to enjoy what they call "Husband's Day" or "Wifey's Day," where pleasurable "training" is bestowed on the privileged one of the week.

That particular day was Ai's. So, three distinctive remaining acts must take place in the following order: upstairs, he would finish up his task of undressing her, literally shower her, and make "make" love when, how, and location of her choosing! So she set those days erotic milestones, and so her husband executed each of them. That cycle repeats itself weekly and gives equal opportunity for both until the end. What not to love?

What's the takeaway from reviewing Ai and Alex's life story? "Many men or women seem to prefer to live together but hesitate to tie up the knot, fearing marriage will ruin the relationship of countless of those who finally got married, for they become practically sexual strangers. They're either up all night taking care of kids or glued to their separate portable electronic devices, binge-watching who knows what nowadays. Some other partners mindlessly but virtually live the famously 'desperate housewives' and other celebrities' lives while failing to appreciate and enjoy the person right under their own roof! So they're exhausted all the time because such mundane activities took every sexual impulse they had out of them. Obviously, that reality is far from how they envisioned their marital life.

Probably their original idea of marriage was to have sex on the kitchen floor, on the stairs, in the shower, inside their cars, or at any other exotic locations ... and not to worry about kids walking in or about modern technology interfering with such vital activities. Single folks fantasize that their future partner would take them to places that wouldn't be human! However, at some point, they would have an epiphany, realizing they are indeed stuck in a relationship with little or no consortium where their kitchen floor or any other exotic spots remain, needlessly, as cold as Italian ceramic tiles ... As a result, they become emotionally depleted, creating an infidelity-prone environment!

In the vast spectrum of relationships, there exists a paradigm that defies convention, exemplified by couples like Ai and Alex. They epitomize a deliberate choice to traverse an alternative path in their family and sex lives—a journey akin to admiring ever-changing scenery, rich with novelty and surprise. Like seasoned companions, they engage in open, uninhibited dialogue, free from the constraints of societal taboos.

Within their dynamic, each partner fulfills the needs of the other, forging a pact that ensures mutual fulfillment. Their approach prompts reflection: In the realm of marriage or impending matrimony, do we align more with the "Use what you got to get what you want" attitude in the likes of Qatar or as resourceful Congo but yet unfulfilled? This inquiry beckons introspection and demands unflinching honesty—a prerequisite for navigating the complexities of intimate relationships.

Amidst a landscape where many couples succumb to erratic behavior, the notion of strategic commitment emerges as a potential antidote to such tumult. Perhaps, by adopting a more intentional approach to partnership, we can mitigate the chaos of misplaced priorities.

Yet, the query persists: Are we inclined to deflect blame outwardly, perpetuating a cycle of relational discord? The introspection urged by Ai and Alex's example invites us to confront our tendencies and consider the implications of our choices.

In essence, their story serves as a beacon, illuminating the transformative power of conscious decision-making in matters of human relationships, marriage above all. By embracing the ethos of mutual understanding and proactive engagement, we may chart a course toward fulfillment and stability in our own relationships—a journey characterized by harmony rather than discord.

Chapter 15
Human Made Disturbance

The convergence of our desires, beliefs, and obligations is a rarity in the complexities of family dynamics. Why is this so? Primarily, its rareness stems from our inherent human nature that often leads to the fluctuation and occasional conflict within the rivers of our expectations. Furthermore, the virtue of patience, though invaluable, is frequently overlooked in our education and upbringing, rendering the act of waiting for a challenging and sometimes debilitating endeavor when faced with deferred realities.

Within the context of marriage, partners are often entrenched in their perceptions and biases, clinging to them until they become untenable. When confronted with the boundaries of their beliefs, they may find themselves resistant to progress, preferring to remain stagnant rather than embracing change. Additionally, the erosion of moral standards within society has led to a lack of stigma surrounding unethical behavior. Commitment and integrity, once esteemed virtues, now hold little sway in certain circles, leading individuals to abandon them at the first sign of societal pressure. For, in the mind of the folks, 'what is sauce for the goose is sauce for the gander.'

What safeguards can prevent us from succumbing to misbehavior in the face of life's intersections? The answer lies in cultivating an elastic mind and a balanced brain. Such attributes enable us to navigate the complexities of familial relationships with adaptability and grace, allowing for the harmonious coexistence of our desires, beliefs, and obligations. By embracing patience, challenging our perceptions, and upholding moral integrity, we can strive to foster healthier and more fulfilling connections within our families and communities.

Researchers have delved into the fascinating realm of cerebral composition, discovering a remarkable attribute among individuals possessing what they term "type one" brains. These individuals exhibit an innate ability for their cognitive faculties to spontaneously revert to their original form following any manner of contraction, dilatation, or distortion. This phenomenon manifests practically as an enhanced capacity for focus, flexibility, and emotional stability within their minds. As a result, they are better equipped to confront and navigate life's myriad uncertainties with resilience and composure.

Consider, for instance, the portrait of a devoted husband and father who exemplifies the virtues associated with such cognitive resilience. Together with his equally dedicated wife, he diligently tends to the needs of their family, ensuring not only the maintenance of their home but also serving as a commendable role model for their two children. With unwavering devotion, he attends to his wife's emotional, spiritual, and intimate desires, embodying the ethos of a modern-day Boy Scout, ever prepared to lend a helping hand.

Furthermore, this exemplary figure demonstrates a commitment to enriching the lives of his loved ones through shared experiences and cherished memories. Year after year, he orchestrates family vacations to destinations chosen with the collective interests in mind, fostering bonds and creating opportunities for exploration and growth. It is no wonder that Megan, his adoring wife, fondly reminisces about her beloved husband whenever prompted to recount their serendipitous meeting.

Indeed, the Roberts story is a testament to the profound impact of emotional intelligence and cognitive resilience in shaping individual lives and familial relationships. In his steadfast dedication and unwavering commitment, we find a compelling embodiment of the enduring values that enrich and sustain the fabric of our society.

Now, just think that one day, Roberts came home from work and found that his wife didn't cook and then had forgotten to order his dinner, as she promised him that she would do. She devoted an awful amount of time and energy to her hair or any other stuff related to feminine upkeep that afternoon! Could you even fathom that he would be so pissed off as to refrain from "helping" his wife around the house for days or weeks? "Of course not!" one might say. And rightly so. Nowadays, mothers wear so many hats on any given day, and any reasonable husband could understand that something may easily slip off from his wife's mind despite her good intentions, even something as crucial as ordering his food, right? Therefore, Roberts went to the kitchen to concoct a "meal" and happily called it a night—end of the story. At first, he was a bit frustrated when realizing his wife's *faux pas*. In evaluating the situation from a holistic perspective, it becomes evident that he can maintain a sense of proportionality, benefiting himself and his entire family unit. By adopting this approach, he demonstrates a commendable level of maturity and consideration for the well-being of those around him. This capacity to prioritize collective welfare underscores his sense of responsibility and resilience in navigating familial dynamics. Consequently, his actions reflect a commitment to fostering harmony and equilibrium within the domestic framework, thus contributing to a cohesive and supportive environment for all involved parties.

In the realm of capitalism, a French saying goes, "*Quand le bâtiment va, tout va,*" which translates to "When construction is booming, everything is going well." Similarly, a saying about family dynamics suggests, "When the wife is pleased, everything flows peacefully and smoothly." This sentiment resonated deeply with Megan one evening when she was pleased with her husband's reaction. The ripple effect was palpable as Megan and her husband seamlessly transitioned into a harmonious evening, assisting their children with homework without a hint of discord. After this productive session, the family relished some cherished quality time together before tucking the kids into bed.

Later, Megan eagerly shared the intricacies of her day with her husband, Roberts. Astutely attuned to the subtleties of their relationship, Roberts listened with genuine interest, hanging onto every word Megan divulged. He skillfully navigated the conversation, prompting Megan to delve deeper into certain aspects, showcasing his attentive nature. Megan couldn't help but wonder if her husband had ulterior motives behind his unwavering attention, but she brushed off her suspicions, knowing deep down that her decision to confide in him was made long before Roberts lent his attentive ear.

In the quiet intimacy of their shared space, Megan, feeling grateful for her husband's understanding and support, sought to express her appreciation meaningfully. And so, as the night unfolded, her gesture of gratitude took a more intimate turn, culminating in a shared moment of affection and passion between husband and wife. Needless to say, the evening ended with Megan and Roberts basking in the warmth of their bond, having navigated the intricacies of their relationship with grace and affection.

Nowadays, people need a drama-free family environment. Why is it so vital? Husbands try to make a living in stress-laden workplaces. Wives are stretched thin with all kinds of responsibilities. The youth is going through a generational crisis with an unprecedented level of sadness and hopelessness, only made worse by the isolation and stress of the COVID-19 pandemic. Parenting is so challenging because a decaying society vies to undo the training that it provides. Thus, the family's structure is the last refuge to give and receive love, affection, support, training, and recovery from the wear and tear of living in this world. When families fail to fulfill such fundamental roles, then society as a whole suffers terribly. For a family, survival no longer depends on any tangible advantage but rather on its members' relative brain type effect. How so?

Compartmentalization is key to avoiding avoidable pitfalls of family life. Without it, there would be no lasting or peaceful matrimony. Like rust to unprotected metals, negative emotions will eat away the fabric of any healthy relationships. Also, hoarding personal or family disappointments and other negative feelings instead of intelligently sorting them out takes up so much of a person's valuable heart and mind space. Then, that will alter their perception, judgments, and outlook on life, ultimately causing them to cease to enjoy and appreciate what they once loved. Finally, fat buildup in the arteries prevents blood from playing its vital role in the body. Likewise, the inability to sift through the imperfections of others and our own shortcomings will sap our ability to play our roles within the family circle. "My husband forgot to buy me flowers for our wedding anniversary or something like that. Therefore, he rightly deserves the silent treatment this weekend," stated one emotionally walloped lady! Unfortunately, many married folks somehow adopted such an approach as a life's principle. But, really, couldn't family members find a better approach to deal with such failings?

To illustrate, let's think about a soccer team during a match. As you may know, each playing team has eleven players on the field, divided into four central positional units: the goalkeeper, the defensive players, the midfielders, and the strikers. So, the keeper protects the goalie. The defensive players provide the first line of defense against the other team's strikers. The midfielders hold the ball to create an opportunity for their strikers to put the ball into the opposing team's goalie. However, even though each group has well-defined roles during a game, all should be willing to do any necessary task within the rules as the game progresses for the team to achieve victory ultimately. Would it be acceptable, under any circumstances, for a goalkeeper to reason that because a striker failed to convert a good opportunity to score, he would altogether stop defending his goalie until he scores a goal? It would be pure insanity, right? Any team with players with such a mentality will never succeed on the pitch and forget about winning championships!

What is true for sports teams also holds true for families. The family unit is like a team where husbands, fathers, wives, mothers, children, and others have well-defined responsibilities but have the same overall goals. True, there will be no physical trophies to be won. However, all should play their roles well and be willing to do whatever is necessary for the family's overall well-being. Each member should be as effective in doing their part and as supportive of their family members as possible. They should be willing to cover for each other when one fails or falls during the match of life.

Moreover, all should create what we will call a "Trust Credit" on each other's name. Practically, it means using what you know about your family to extend the extra privilege to each of them without extra prerequisites, trusting they won't abuse or disappoint you. However, when the latter does happen, you will be willing to debit some trust from their "Trust Credit" account to cover it. So everyone should strive daily to build up their own "trust credit" by treating each other with love and respect.

For, absolutely, no one will NEVER have unlimited trust! But when each family member has enough of it to sprinkle over when life does happen, ultimately, all will feel loved, respected, and motivated to keep playing their respective roles. Similarly, a teammate's error may cause a team to initially trail on the scoreboard but win the match afterward when all the players put in a determined effort. That kind of team mentality is what all expect from any functioning family, right?

A husband or a wife has to be able to, after combing through life's events, identify what is important and then make a conscientious effort to keep defending and even cherish it. Life, as we know it, is definitely a frustrating, vexing mixed bag, especially for married gents. So each time they come to a disappointing intersection, one has to decide what's the best course of action: ignoring the rest of the traffic and crashing it all or making a reasonable turn to a chosen destination. Unable to let go of resentment, some refuse to forgive the imperfect partner they swore "to love until life sets them apart!" Others, self-absorbed due to the so-called midlife crisis, would develop a disorder named anhedonia that is always detrimental to any relationship.

Consequently, at some point in their journey, all those people realize that married life isn't going to be as rosy or thornless as they had hoped for. But unfortunately, they seem to be allergic to compartmentalization, a remedy that could have helped them to digest their partners' shortcomings. Therefore, how many smart folks who should have known better decide anyway to throw it all away, often just for the sake of having reason or being in the right?

Chapter 16
The Long Way To The Storm

The phenomenon known as "Until it's Gone Syndrome" appears to be increasingly prevalent among many individuals today, affecting both men and women. In the pursuit of what they deem to be "suitable" partners, individuals invest significant effort, only to swiftly discard these precious connections at the first sign of marital discord. Roxye found herself caught in this pattern. Growing up amidst a complex familial dynamic, she experienced a childhood shaped by her father's transient relationships, where stability was a fleeting concept. Her father, Bobby, whose numerous offspring were scattered across different continents, including Roxye, Chesty, and Carlexa, had a penchant for uprooting lives and relocating. Due to his geographic mobility, Bobby's relationships with his children's mothers remained distant or non-existent, tethered to a distant Caribbean country. Roxye and her siblings found themselves transplanted to the United States, where Bobby's latest female companion, considerably younger, assumed a maternal role, blurring the lines of familial boundaries. In an attempt to provide some semblance of stability, Bobby secured accommodation in a suburban enclave near Washington, D.C., setting the stage for Roxye's journey amidst the complexities of familial relationships and cultural displacement.

Bobby's children epitomized resilience in the face of adversity. Banding together, they forged a path to thrive amidst their new circumstances. Recognizing the pivotal role education played in securing a stable future in their adopted homeland, they approached their studies with unwavering determination. Graduating from both high school and college marked significant milestones in their journey. Today, several of the sons proudly serve in the ranks of the US Army, embodying a commitment to duty and service. Meanwhile, the daughters pursued careers that provided financial security and addressed fundamental human needs, as outlined by Maslow's hierarchy. With their professional lives established, thoughts turned to building families of their own, contingent upon finding partners who could complement their aspirations. Yet, amid societal pressures and shifting norms, lingered the question: could they resist the insidious pull of a disposable culture that threatens familial bonds? Do individuals possess the capacity to defy ingrained patterns, transcending the limitations imposed by their environment? These pressing inquiries underscore the complexity of human nature and the perpetual quest for personal evolution.

Roxye had transformed remarkably, blossoming into a highly productive young woman. Her sense of fulfillment emanated from her chosen career path within the US national government. With a sharp intellect and a deep passion for her work, Roxye found immense joy in contributing to her country's welfare. Moreover, she dedicated much of her free time to volunteer work at her local church, a commitment that underscored her compassionate nature.

Despite her achievements and contentment in her professional and philanthropic endeavors, Roxye confided in her friends about a lingering desire for companionship. She yearned for the presence of "Mr. Right" in her life, someone who shared her faith and with whom she could envision building a family. To Roxye, compatibility in faith and aspirations for parenthood were non-negotiable qualities in her quest for a lifelong partner.

In her characteristic resolve, Roxye firmly believed that challenges should be met head-on, employing the resources at hand. She often quoted her mantra, "One should hit a barking dog with the weapon that he/she has," reflecting her pragmatic approach to overcoming obstacles in life.

Roxye has found herself nervous about her marriage prospects at times. She was approaching her thirties. Her awareness of her biological clock was becoming more acute. In her mind, it was ticking like a timer in a timed bomb that could explode at any time. To her, instead of inflicting some structural damage, it would smash or reduce her chance to attract Mr. Right before it's too late. She felt powerless, even a bit desperate at times. Although she still lived with her siblings, Roxye longed for a more intimate relationship. They assumed she was out of the woods because of her professional success, but her intermittent loneliness was real.

Her sisters may perceive Roxye as a straightforward, churchgoing individual, yet beneath this facade lies a woman of intricate depth. While she values a partner who shares her faith, this isn't to say she imposes dogma onto others. Roxye seeks a husband, but her tolerance for discrimination is minimal, a non-negotiable aspect of her character. Indeed, she's devoutly religious, but her priorities lean more toward fulfilling her emotional needs rather than solely seeking divine approval. In her perspective, the rhythm of divine judgment operates on a different time scale compared to her own.

Furthermore, Roxye's mindset echoes that of the evangelical pastor in "Coming to America I," who skillfully suggested that even the most unconverted could succumb to the persuasive allure of faith, especially when presented with a captivating proposition. Roxye firmly believes in the seductive power of her presence, akin to a temple drawing in the faithful. While some religious denominations employ music, dance, or even chicken soup to attract souls to the Lord, Roxye ponders if her allurements might be the bait to attract the right man.

Some believe time is the essence of our character. Others opine that it's instead one's infancy that constantly runs through his veins. Still, Roxye always thought all the decisions a person ever made determine who he really is. Therefore, during one of her emotional rut moments of late, she reviewed some of the important ones. On one hand, Roxye realized that some of her decisions were final. On the other hand, she was wondering if it was still possible to revoke or modify others made during her youth back home many years ago.

Roxye was in an emotional rut. Nobody seemed to understand; not even she couldn't explain why she randomly felt so sad and lonely lately despite having so many other things to be grateful for, and apparently, there was no man out there fitting to rescue her either. In that state of mind, Roxye mentally reviewed all ex-boyfriends and "former unworthy wannabes. ' One of Roxye's regretted decisions concerned a young man named David Clarke, whom she knew back home in Barbados before immigrating into the U.S.

Deep within, Roxye felt trapped in her conundrum. It has been said to take refuge in the memory lane when reality is helpless and hopeless. We all have a love we can't forget, one that our soul is anchored to for better or worse. So that weekend, again, Roxye couldn't stop thinking about David, with whom she was infatuated in her girlhood. Their parents lived in the same neighborhood. As a young girl, she used to see him in some of her dreams. Her feminine sense told her that he probably liked her. But his young age and his shyness prevented him from expressing his romantic feelings for her. "If only I was as bold then as 1 become now…" Roxye mentally reasoned. Her cold soul kept wondering about whatever had ever happened to him. Is he still alive? Does he still live back home? Is he married with kids? What are the chances that he is still available…"

Roxye smiled, realizing how ridiculous these questions were. Nevertheless, she felt a little better right away because the last idea had given her hope, however minute. Thus, knowing well that even crazy monkeys are afraid of their reflection, discreetly, Roxye decided to inquire about David's whereabouts, just in case … However, she started by asking David's old friends and his old neighbors, but not David's family or her own family, anticipating their weird looks and uncomfortable questions that she wanted to avoid early on.

During their conversation, one of David's former schoolmates casually mentioned that he believed David was still residing in Barbados. "I can't say for certain if he's tied the knot, but here's Sam's cell number," he offered in response to Roxye's persistent inquiry about David's whereabouts. Armed with this newfound contact information for David's brother, Roxye found herself on the cusp of unraveling the mysteries she'd been chasing. Yet, strangely, instead of feeling immediate relief, she was overcome with an unexpected wave of anxiety. She had become a player in a high-stakes poker game, desperately seeking that one elusive card to complete her hand. But, like a player hesitating to reveal their final card, she hesitated to dial the number, fearing what the outcome might be. In this moment of hesitation, she found solace in the illusion of control that delayed the inevitable provided. It was as if by prolonging the suspense, she could also extend her hope and ward off any potential disappointment. But as the saying goes, you can only keep a "knowable mystery" shrouded in mystery for so long before reality inevitably catches up with you.

Roxye was on a mission to track down David. First, she concocted a story to find out David's marital status without raising Sam's suspicion about her true motive. " But he no longer lives in Holetown. After secondary school, David moved to Bridgetown for college. Right after graduating, he started working for the city," Sam told Roxye. "Can we have David's contact information? "Freddy," one of his old classmates, would like to reconnect with him," she smoothly asked Sam. While they were still on the phone, the sound of Sam's text message made her smile. She promised to pass his brother's information to a fictitious Freddy, and then they hung up. Finally, she set her mind on fire to devise 'the right reason' to fly to Bridgetown, Barbados, to squash her family's potentially many intrusive questions.

Even though her mother lived back home at that time, she never went there to visit her. Roxye was the sort of person who appeared to "divorce" her Caribbean roots after securing some material well-being in the U.S. "What...? You are going where...? Did we hear you correctly...? Are you, Roxye, planning to go to Barbados to visit your mom? Why now? Is there something that you aren't telling us..?" Chesty and Carlexa shouted at Roxye after telling her plan, as she expected that they would.

David had entrenched himself firmly within Roxye's thoughts for the past several weeks, exerting a comforting placebo effect. Despite their lack of direct contact, the mere presence of romantic hope and possibilities infused her mind and heart, filling the previously vacant spaces. With his image lingering in her consciousness, her days seemed to shrink in duration, and her weekends became more manageable, buoyed by the anticipation of what could be. This transformation didn't escape the notice of those around her. Whispers of speculation arose within her household and congregation, attempting to attribute her newfound contentment to various causes. Some suggested it might be the "Barbados dual effect," as her upcoming trip to the island loomed on the horizon. Others of a more spiritual inclination interpreted it as a manifestation of divine grace, believing that the Lord's light was shining upon her. Observers within her church community noted Roxye's heightened engagement during the pastor's sermons, followed by a discernible uplift in her demeanor after that. An old friend once remarked, "It's only the dogs that know what we say in our prayers." Surely, Roxye could resonate with this sentiment, silently acknowledging the unspoken prayers that danced within her heart.

Chesty and Carlexa were still in disbelief on their way to the airport, despite Roxye's latest explanation about missing her mom or about COVID-19 travel restrictions being lifted as being the real motive that she wanted to go back home for the first time. They didn't buy any of it! Perplexed but clueless, they kept their ears on the ground, especially after hugging their sister's goodbyes before she went through airport security. As for Roxye, she clearly knew why she flew from DCA to BGI. Her heart was after the man she dreamt about as a young girl years ago. However, she felt a bit uneasy while up in the sky, realizing how uncertain and worldlike her endeavor was. But the relentless tickings from her biological clock were much louder than her dwarfed "Christian" conscience. Soon, she will be landed in

Barbados, where her mother Clarissa and her cousin John will come to pick her up.

Roxye's time on the island was literally numbered. John, his cousin and local private investigator, has already found out where David lives in town. She was relieved upon learning his bachelor's status and his willingness to meet her later that day. So, the following morning, all Roxye could think about was her upcoming encounter with him. In fact, ever since her flight was booked, Roxye had been racking her brain to select a perfect fit, feminine enough to make the "kill" or, at least, entice her prized "prey." So, in her mind, modesty was out of the question! Unfortunately, her extensive shopping back in the States before the trip didn't make things any easier. However, it was decision time because Roxye realized the option of wearing Eve's original outfit was too soon!

Women often dress their feelings. For her first encounter with David after many years, Roxye opted for casus belli rather than for appeasement, wearing a modern burgundy asymmetrical cutout jumpsuit cut from a stretch fabric and has a figure-hugging contour that underscores her generous curves. 'Elle voulait le frapper très fort!' Even though she knew, through her cousin's informant, that things were skewed in her favor, Roxye didn't want to take any chance; it was about that time to have her own man in her life, and David was it. So, like a risk-averse military strategist, Roxye's main goal was to overwhelm David's heart. One way to attain it was to mitigate any likely resistance or possible hesitations. David knew why his old childhood girlfriend was in town. But he was in for a surprise as to how determined Roxye was to renew their romantic friendship!

Chapter 17
When the North Atlantic Ocean Reconnects with the Caribbean Sea

As instructed, Dinah, David's little niece, opened the front door and led Roxye to her uncle's backyard. It was serene, romantically set up with her in mind.

"Hello 'Stranger!' Long time no see," Roxye tightly hugged David with a broad smile.

"Roxye... you look superb! Please make yourself home! It's great seeing you! I thought the States had made you forget about *us*!" uttered an excited David. After they settled down, Dinah served them flying fish dishes and coconut water, peach keen drinks as they dived into their life's life-altering conversations.

"I didn't know what to make out of it when Sam told me about an obscure old classmate inquiring about my whereabouts," David said as he sipped his drink.

"... And then a few days later, John mentioned your own query ... Now that you're here, my curiosity peaked, wondering if there was any connection," continued David as he observed Roxye's smiles amusingly.

"Thanks. You aren't bad yourself. You're fresh to death," said she, returning his compliments.

"Thanks. We are getting by here!" He humbly replied.

"Please, tell me all you have done since you left here. Yeah, how does life abroad treat you?" an impatient David finally asked.

"Well, well! Where shall we start? All right! Let's say that I have done all an immigrant young girl ought to do in order to make it out in the States. But, even after finding God there, I came to realize that what I needed the most in my life wasn't there!" Roxye answered matter-of-factly.

"No surprise you made it all right in the Land of Opportunities. I have known you to be a smart and studious girl. But I am a bit puzzled by the latter part of your answer. What do you mean by it?" David wanted to know.

"I suspect you might already know the answer to your question … But I do understand you may want confirmation directly from me after many years. So please take my presence here as a token of it. Before going further, I wanted to make sure of what is left between us, considering the time that has elapsed," Roxye responded without answering him directly.

"Well, you returned when I least expected you; however, heavens know the timing is just right. I am not a kid anymore. Do you know what I mean? So, I am not oblivious to the possible meaning of your gesture, but I didn't want to be presumptuous either. What I felt in my heart for you since the beginning remained something I came to treasure even after you had left the island. I often thought of reaching out to you, but I feared your family might misconstrue my intentions. You are aware of how folks here think about these kinds of things. But I know about you from afar, so to speak," David explained.

"Oh, David!" Roxye exclaimed, "I do understand. Like gold nuggets, our love needed to pass the test; time needs the purifying power of fire. Now it's clear that our feelings towards each other remained unchanged despite all. In fact, I never really left you. In my soul, I went abroad with you, for our love stays hidden in the innermost part of my heart. What I saw and lived in the States instinctively kept bringing me back to it. So, as you said earlier, I am no longer a little girl in love, either. I knew what to do and finally did what a woman in love usually does …"

"Does that mean that you have contacted my brother to inquire about my whereabouts while pretending to be doing so on behalf of a so-called classmate?" pushed David, giving another occasion to come clean.

"Yes, it was all me all along and all for my own sanity! Culturally, I was venturing into forbidden territory. So I wasn't too thrilled putting my reputation on the Island chopping board, then! You're fully aware of how our people consider such initiatives by a woman. Aren't you? Didn't you just say that you stayed apprised also of my life, albeit indirectly? It's done! Now that I have found you! Rest assured that, at my age, I wasn't taking any chances … unless you are upset about my feminine ways," she frankly replied with a seductive smile!

"No worries! You are the kind of girl who isn't afraid of going after what's important to her. So, even if I were, your smile always has an overpowering effect on me. As always, It fills me with all kinds of inhuman ideas or desires ...," said the pensive gentleman across the table.

"LOL! David!" cried out Roxye, "are ... you serious?"

"Yeah! That's the way I feel right now. I know I can be straightforward, as you always wanted me to, whenever I am with you. Does it still hold water?" he quickly asked, making sure that a faux pas didn't disturb the wonderful dinner he was having with his beautiful girlfriend of old.

"Of course! I always want to know what you think and how you feel. Rest assured that you don't desire anything that is foreign to me, especially for a born-again virgin ... except ..., as such, you might have to be a little patient here until we ... You know what I mean?" she said without any firm conviction.

David's response was laced with a playful tone, his words dancing between affection and a hint of impatience. "No, no! I understand, but my flesh won't always agree, especially when we share the same geographic location! My Roxye, I love you no matter how long I have to wait again ... I am kidding! I can't wait that long unless you would like me to burn up in my lust! Do you remember how long you had me wait before the first time we ...?" His words trailed off, leaving an open space for reminiscence.

Roxye's reply carried a sense of fondness tinged with humor as she indulged in the banter. "Oh, you are so sweet and understanding! But I better call John for my ride home before your charm overpowers whatever is left of my will!" Her acquiescence hinted at a shared understanding, a familiarity with David's persuasive charm.

David's offer to drive her home was a practical solution and a gesture of consideration. "It's already past nine! Time seems to fly whenever I am with you! I can drive you home. How long are you on the island for? Have you toured it yet? I know the best places that you would like to see. I will take tomorrow off if you are up for it. What do you say?" His words carried a sense of excitement, a readiness to extend their time together beyond the present moment. The offer was not just about transportation but an invitation to explore and create shared experiences, showcasing his thoughtfulness and eagerness to deepen their connection.

"Oh! Thank you. It's very thoughtful of you. But John is hanging out in the bar down the road; he is coming once I call him; he will take me home. I am here for the rest of the week. Can you pick me up tomorrow morning at 10 at my mom's place?"

"We got another date then," shouted David excitedly.

"I am looking forward to spending more time with you. Thanks again for a lovely evening," Roxye said as John was pulling up in front of David's house.

She hugged and kissed her boyfriend "2.0" on the lips and then got into her cousin's Suzuki Grand Vitara, full of new hope.

Chapter 18
The Heart's Reasons

John eagerly anticipated hearing all the juicy details about his cousin's romantic escapade. The anticipation was palpable as he practically leaned forward in his seat. As soon as Roxye clicked her seatbelt into place, she could sense his impatience radiating from him. With a playful glint in her eye, she wasted no time addressing his curiosity.

"All right, spill it!" John urged, barely able to contain his excitement. "What's the scoop?"

Roxye chuckled at his eagerness. "Ask away, John. I'm an open book."

John hesitated momentarily, a hint of formality creeping into his demeanor. "Shouldn't we observe some formalities?" he suggested tentatively.

Roxye waved off his concern with a casual gesture. "Nah, we're past formalities. Just dive in!"

Curiosity piqued, John dove straight to the heart of the matter. "So, how was it? Did sparks fly? Did you strike romantic gold?"

Roxye leaned back in her own seat then with a wry smile, ready to regale him with the tale. "Honestly, it exceeded expectations. Given the circumstances, we both realized our love couldn't wait any longer. We're ready to take action sooner rather than later."

John's eyes widened in astonishment. "Wow, that's... quite the revelation. So, do you believe your youthful romance has blossomed into something more... practical?"

Roxye considered his question carefully. "Practical? Well, if by practical you mean 'marriage material,' then absolutely. David ticks all the boxes."

John nodded, absorbing her response. "Got it. So, it seems like you've found something real."

Roxye nodded firmly. "Definitely. And I couldn't be happier about it."

"I always enjoy talking with you. You are a straight shooter, too. Now, please tell me, does the fact that David doesn't share your faith give you any pause? In fact, this guy wouldn't set his feet in any churches if it isn't during funerals or weddings!" he pressed on.

Her friend's inquiry cut straight to the heart of the matter, questioning the depth of her convictions and the compatibility of her relationship. The mention of David's disinterest in attending church beyond obligatory events underscored a potential source of conflict, highlighting a fundamental difference in belief systems.

"What about it?" she rhetorically asked, her tone tinged with a hint of defiance. "Shall we start praying now for more folks to die so he could attend church services more often…? John, just think: was I born a Baptist? You know the answer very well. However, it seems that I have a broader definition of proselytism than you do!

Her retort carried a sharp edge, challenging the conventional notions of faith and evangelism. By questioning the sincerity of her friend's concern and sarcastically suggesting a morbid solution to David's church attendance issue, she revealed a deeper layer of frustration with societal expectations and religious norms. The reference to her Baptist upbringing hinted at the complexity of her own spiritual journey, suggesting a departure from traditional dogma in favor of a more inclusive worldview, meaning marrying the one one's heart desired.

"What do you mean, Roxye? I just wanted to have your thoughts on the matter…," he said, sensing a change in her tone.

"Well, salvation comes in many ways. To me, that means it doesn't really matter how a person comes to a place of worship. What's important is what he or she takes out of it afterward. However, at my age, now isn't the time to linger on such things. So let's get him in there first! There you have it! Cousin, I think we both can agree on that, right?" she reasoned.

In this introspective moment, the character probes into the nuanced understanding of salvation, a topic that holds deep significance for many. The notion that the path to worship varies for each individual reflects a broader theme of tolerance and acceptance. This sentiment underscores a mature perspective, suggesting that the outcome of spiritual exploration is what truly matters. However, amidst this contemplation, the urgency of the present moment is not lost, as the character swiftly redirects the conversation, highlighting a pragmatic approach to the situation at hand.

On that last point, John decided to rest his case. He was wise to do so then, for it's often as futile to reason with a wild mule as it is with a woman in love! It's said to be one of the rare phenomena that's beyond the realm of human reason! As he pondered on this fact, Roxye's cell phone rang, breaking the silence. It was Roxye's sisters!

In acknowledging the futility of continuing the debate, John demonstrates a shrewd understanding of human nature, recognizing the inexplicable force of emotions, particularly in matters of the heart. The comparison between reasoning with a wild mule and a woman in love adds a touch of humor yet carries a weight of truth in observing the complexities of interpersonal dynamics. The sudden interruption by Roxye's sisters serves as a catalyst, abruptly shifting the focus of the scene and injecting a sense of immediacy and anticipation into the narrative.

"We knew it, and we knew it! " Chesty and Carlexa said in unison.

The synchronized exclamation from Roxye's sisters adds a layer of camaraderie and familiarity to the interaction, reinforcing the bond between the characters. Their simultaneous declaration hints at a shared history and inside joke, inviting the reader to speculate on the nature of their relationship with Roxye and the context of their anticipation. This brief exchange serves as a bridge to the next phase of the narrative, leaving the reader intrigued and eager to uncover what unfolds next.

"What about 'Hello! How are you, sister?' Roxye asked rhetorically to diffuse what she felt was coming.

"You went back home to rekindle your love affair with David, not really to visit your mom as you wanted us to believe. Isn't it? We got the news from Barbados that you had dinner with him in his backyard!" they explained, never minding her faint request for politeness.

"Ah! That! News travel fast on the island. John and I haven't even gotten home yet. I guess I could have been more straightforward with you girls. I wasn't sure if my old flame was on the market or if he would even be willing to consider such a possibility. So, I kept my intentions under wraps until I saw where things were. Nobody knew why I was in town except my cousin John. By the way, he just said "hello" to you guys," Roxye finally conceded.

"We couldn't believe our eyes when I saw you guys together on social media! First of all, it seems that you're doing things upside down. It should be David who initiated such demarch, not you, girl! Also, even if he did, we believed that you would decline his advances on the basis of religious incompatibility. Aren't you a church girl now?"

When John overheard it, he felt a bit reassured that his earlier questions were valid. He acted like he was focused on the roads but was keenly interested to hear how Roxye would reply. And she did so in a sassy way!

"Seriously, ladies? Entertaining the idea of actively pursuing a man seems like a step in the wrong direction. Doesn't it? After all these years of meticulously following societal norms, patiently waiting for Prince Charming to sweep me off my feet, what do I have to show for it? Absolutely nothing. Now, in my thirties, I find myself with everything I've ever wanted—except the one person I long to share it all with. Still, he remains elusive. Even my own family begins to question if there's something inherently flawed about me. It's baffling. Isn't it? But to you, is the notion of remaining passive somehow the accepted path for a woman? Truly?"

"We never see you like that, big sis! On the contrary, you are our model; we always look up to you. We are just concerned that our folks may call you some undesirable names. You know …, we wonder if that ever crosses your mind?" Carlexa injected before she could finish up her last sentence.

"Of Course! I am a Bajan woman, after all. But my experience and observation have taught me that "Cat luck isn't dog luck." So, I decided to follow a different track. A woman can spend hours upon hours, sometimes hopping from store to store, looking for a particular dress, trying it out to make sure that all is right before deciding to buy it. And we would return all of these stupid outfits in a split second, anyway! Then, when we think about it, is it a colossal cultural blunder for women to play a more active role, all things being equal, in selecting their significant others?" Roxye said to continue reasoning with her sisters.

"We understand. Even better, let's say we agree with you on that, but shouldn't you look for someone within your denomination?" They continued to press further on the matter.

"That's exactly what I have been doing for over a decade! But, so far, in my thirties, all I am left with is what the blind man saw! Are you saying I should stay put until a 'gift-wrapped husband' knocks at my door?" she asked jokingly with a big smile.

"Very funny, Roxye! You must have a romantic breakthrough with David tonight! However, how will he fare once marooned on your own island?" they said, caving in finally to a resourceful Roxye.

"Interesting question, but let's save it for our next conversation. We're arriving at my mom's house now. It's been nice chatting with you both. Good night!" John's voice trailed off as the car fell silent once more.

"You seem pretty convinced about David. Are you planning to discuss him with Tantie or leaving it to word-of-mouth on the island?" John inquired, slipping back into his role as a trusted advisor.

"Mom's pretty laid-back; I'm sure she'll be supportive. But I think it's best if I break the news to her myself," she replied confidently.

"You sound confident, Roxye. I'll leave that in your capable hands," John said, giving her a warm hug before bidding her good night.

David's positive reaction cleared up everything for Roxye. No trouble happened to be found in paradise, to the contrary. Makeup removal routine is necessary for women who constantly need a face to go out with! For her, going through that process that night felt peculiarly rewarding! First, she appreciated how crucial her 'fabricated beauty' had probably played in enfolding David earlier that night. Second, she experienced a sensation often described as a tingling head "orgasm." What not to love! Finally, afterward, she hatched a mental plan with sites and things she wanted to enjoy on the island with her new guy friend. In her mind, nothing will prevent her from giving herself to him… in holy matrimony.

In the middle of it all, her cell phone rang. As one could expect, it was her boyfriend 2.0. Naturally, he wanted to make sure she got home safely. But beyond that, he wanted more of her voice, her smiles, and more of her! Endlessly sharing such things is what nourishes any new romantic love. "I couldn't go to bed without knowing if you got home safe and sound!" he confessed.

"Thank you. Back in the States, that's what I have been missing the most! Someone who personally cared for me! I was getting ready to go to sleep myself. Of course, I planned to check on you before! Were you missing me?" she asked finally to tease him.

"Are you genuinely surprised? 'Rox,' you've reeled me back where I always longed to be. The time we've shared together only intensifies my desire for you even further," lamented David.

"Then, in this case, we're in trouble! What are we gonna do?" she replied, recalling her own earlier experience.

"In trouble… how?" he curiously asked. They both laughed loudly.

"Curious to dive into the depths of memory lane, I found myself unexpectedly stirred. You know the feeling. Last night, your presence ignited a sense of vulnerability within me that felt almost perilous. As for tomorrow, well, I haven't quite devised a foolproof plan yet," she confessed softly, her voice trailing off.

"Very funny! Babe, you need some protection against…your own desires..!" said her beau, trying to help her face her own paradox. As David was talking, he could sense that her dulcinea was dozing on and off on him.

"What did ya say… my love?" mumbled Roxye. That confirmed it all. She needed to rest up after such an exciting night! So he once again professed his love and kissed her good night.

Chapter 19
Interpreting The Warnings

Roxye, thus far immersed in the pursuit of her American Dream, found solace in the bustling distractions around her, now seeking to evade the weight of her solitary contemplations. As she stood on the cusp of realizing her cherished aspiration for marriage, optimism enveloped her for the days ahead. The anticipation for the forthcoming event was palpable, the night preceding it feeling agonizingly short. As morning dawned, thoughts of David monopolized Roxye's mind as she prepared for her significant milestone. Seeking reassurance, she had enlisted her cousin John as their appointed chaperone the previous evening. Expecting David's arrival at ten, Roxye's anxiety dissolved into relief when John finally signaled the approach of his beloved's car, albeit fashionably late, at nearly eleven twenty-three.

When Roxye saw David, she felt as excited as a kid who had just seen the ice cream truck approaching his house during the Summer! She ran toward him and jumped on him like they had never seen each other for a long time! Afterward, John, when shown his watch in disbelief, David, like most of his fellow Barjans, had "an ever-ready plaster fuh his lateness." John didn't do anything out of it; "Life happened!" After the new boyfriend went inside to greet his future mother-in-law and associates, as Roxys had suggested, the trio were finally on their way to visit the Garrison Historic Area.

Both gentlemen finally agreed there was plenty to see and to do there. As for Roxye, like a tourist with a trusted guide, she was willing to go anywhere on the island as long as David was at the party. So she nodded her approbation just as a formality. Thus, they went to visit both the historic George Washington House and the Savannah Garrison. All that walking and talking made a hole in their stomach. David suggested they stop at the George Washington Coffee House to grab something to eat, but Pebbles Beach was their final destination for the day. It's one of John's favorite spots to cool down after visiting the district.

As her cousin was securing beach chairs and amenities for all of them, Roxye grabbed David away for a romantic walk along the beach lines. She didn't want this first opportunity for anything in the world. Besides, she felt as comfortably sexy in her one-piece bathing suit as the fishes in their elements. David reclaimed his role as a sole personal guide and decided to keep his prized, attractive girlfriend tightly close to his side as if she were blind! Since she left the island in her early teens, David kept pointing out different things that he thought might interest her, such as the ritual of daily horses racing on the beach or how often so many cruise ships docked in the city port during this time of the year. "I feel happy being here with you, my love," an overwhelmed Roxye finally confessed. The gentleman's voice deepened noticeably, occasionally faltering in an embarrassingly cracked manner, a result of his body's release of testosterone and adrenaline hormones.

She later confided in a colleague's girlfriend when she got to the States. "I felt a throbbing between my legs as sexual energy was pulsing back and forth through David's bare skin, rubbing on mine during each step we took during our beach stroll. But I couldn't dare share such a disturbing fact with him because I wasn't oblivious to its effect on him, too!"

David's hot pressing issues were compounded by Roxye's good-looking, beachy derriere thirst-trapping many of his fellow compatriots. They could see she was a true Bayan taxed with visible, added exotic finesse. Roxye's ensemble was so enchanted that they failed to see her boyfriend next to her. Others resorted to catcalling her while gesturing inappropriately. "Can I put my aloe vera on you?' shouted one of them. Despite David's repeated protests and calls for them to stop, their excitement barely died off. Finally, he suggested they head back to find John's station. They have seen him sipping a refreshing glass of mauby to quench his thirst and cool himself down. What just happened gave Roxye an extra reason to have a man in her life! "At last, my stag life is nearing its end!" she reflected on herself.

As David went to the bar to fetch some drinks for his belle, John found himself alone with his visiting cousin for the first time since they left the house. "I apologize for the unpleasant encounter with those individuals on the beach. The allure of rare beauty can sometimes unsettle us men, especially women like you. Thankfully, you had David with you; it could have been much worse if you were alone … How you feelin'?"

"I was baffled, especially when they kept going despite David's efforts to stop it, but I wasn't too afraid. Thanks! for the compliment, too. But do you think that I am that pretty, though? Are you saying it because you're my cousin? Be honest!" inquired Roxye as she sat on the beach chair, looking at the infinite horizon.

"Truly, There is nothing homely about you. Look at you in this Bikini! He has been baked, alive! Please don't tell me you're unaware of the torture you have been putting David through ever since he picked us up this morning! We heard that you're going to church now. You're leaving in a couple of days, right? What's your plan for his "ongoing male issues?"

"Did he tell you anything…It's hard for me, too. I don't even remember the last time that I … That was the main reason I asked you to be with us today as our chaperone. I love him but love the Lord more. I want to give myself to him after holy matrimony …" Roxye said with anguish.

"Check this up! A friend of mine who belongs to the same denomination as you. He had a girlfriend. He told us that since they are in a committed relationship, it's ok to do the deed. "But, we pray for the Lord's forgiveness after each time that we did it!" he affirmed when we tried to paint him as a hypocrite. How would you describe your relationship with David, a heathen? I know that he is crazy for you! Would that pass the smell test in your church?" John continued to put the pressure on her.

"Oh, John! They were going to do it! Don't they realize they can't have a church wedding if she gets pregnant? As for me, I want to marry David. In fact, I already see him as the father of my future children," she replied, feeling a sudden rush of heat.

"Does that mean you might be open to being intimate before legally tying the knot?" John inquired, seeking clarification.

"What paperwork are you referring to? Are you married to Julia, the mother of your son? And what about Isaac from the Bible? Did he sign any paperwork when he took Rebekah into his mother's tent?" Roxye retorted, her agitation evident.

"I guess you may have a point. I was just wondering," conceded John, sensing that the conversation had run its course. Even though he wanted to ask her cousin, "How would she manage the inevitable tension they will face during the transitional period after snatching David off the island?" But, not wanting to sour his relationship with his cousin, John decided to let it drop.

Upon seeing David coming, Roxye jumped out of her chair and ran toward him. "You came back just in time because I was about to call 911 thinking maybe a mean beach girl stole you away at the bar," she flirtingly said.

"There was a line. I wanted to make sure you were done right. Do you like it?" the caring boyfriend replied.

Roxye nodded in agreement, indicating her willingness to play along. Feigning discomfort as if she had trodden on a sharp object, Roxye requested to be transported to her chair on David's back. David acquiesced without hesitation. "That was the easiest load I've ever borne," David recounted to his friends afterward.

When the couple arrived at their chairs, John was already in the water, so they joined him there. They stayed in for about an hour; it was a pleasant sunny day, and the water was nice and calm. They swam back and forth to see who was the fastest among them. "John was," they both finally admitted. John suggested that they head back home because he had to visit Julia's ailing uncle with her that afternoon. For some reason, David wanted to stay longer, alone with his girl! But Roxye reasoned that it would be best if they all left together as they came. She was worried about giving her folks extra ground for gossiping about her. Also, she didn't want to have that kind of conversation with her traditional mother when she found out that she and David remained on the beach alone after her cousin had left.

David finally dropped them off and went home, pleased about how well his day went. John went to take care of his family business. As for Roxye, she needed to manage some women's business before joining her family for dinner. "You have been spending an awful amount of time with David! As if you came here just to be with him! It seems we were mistakenly thinking that you grew out of whatever you felt for him," snapped Clarissa, Roxye's mother, at her daughter's first opportunity.

"Mom! I thought so, too, for a long time! But you know how hard it could be to forget about our first love! I couldn't find a better one in the States, not for lack of trying. And, like nature, our hearts abhor a vacuum! So inevitably, mine recoiled back to where love once flourished," Roxye poured out her heart, looking for just a little understanding from her mother.

"If it is true, it must be terrifying for serious young women there who aspire to matrimony! Love doesn't grow over there? Is it *really* a no-love's land?" asked a more sympathetic Clarissa.

"To the contrary, mom! Like weeds, love seems to outgrow anything else. There is plenty of it! But unfortunately, it's the cheap one, the weedy kind. The lava love! Therefore, a real, responsible, and enduring one seems to be buried by it or even outdated. And, unfortunately, I have known both to appreciate the difference." explained her daughter patiently.

"I see. Thanks for helping us to peek into that unseemly void! On the other hand, in the past, you have always found infinite excuses not to visit us here. But to rekindle your fling with David, gee, here you are! But we barely see you! So you really think that he is the real deal, don't you?" said Clarissa as she repackaged her original complaint.

"I've missed you, Mom. So, eventually, I made the trip to visit you and brought David along. Our relationship has evolved beyond a mere fling; it's become serious. We're starting to think about our future... David brings me immense joy. I genuinely love him," Roxye confided earnestly, hinting at the prospect of marriage.

Their heartfelt conversation, mother to daughter, left them both longing for more. Clarissa was taken aback by Roxye's readiness to contemplate marriage, but being the shrewd mother she was when it came to her daughter's happiness, she reassured Roxye of her unwavering support. In exchange, Roxye agreed to spend the following day at home, aiming to end her mother's sporadic lectures. Sensing her mother's satisfaction, Roxye suggested having dinner with David and a few siblings, to which her mother readily agreed. With everything settled, Roxye tended to her personal grooming before retiring for the night, fulfilling her promise to call David, who had eagerly awaited her update throughout her conversation with her mother. He intently listened as she recounted their discussion, expressing his love until the late hours of the night.

Ever since she got on the island, it has become Roxye's routine to wake up naturally, without the help of any modern machine, be it electronic or biological. Yesterday was just a perfect day for her: everything started to fall into place. So she slept like a log! She woke up past eleven in the morning. She felt rejuvenated. Roxye was reviewing its piles of unread messages, replying to some while eating her brunch. Clarissa once jokingly wondered if her daughter used her cell phone to breathe or stay alive because she always seemed glued to it! Once the dinner table was cleared, she went back into her room. First thing first. She WhatsApped her sisters to remind them that her return flight was in two days. Then she called David. They talked for nearly two hours. "Babe, I can't wait to see you here tonight. I still don't know what clothes to wear! But I want to be and look sexy just for you ... if you promise that you will know how to behave... All of that being said, how would you dress me tonight?" she finally said to tease him.

"Same here! Thanks love. I don't have the mastery of myself while in your presence. So, frankly, I can't promise anything! As for my input, you don't really need it because beauty and sexiness are, first of all, symmetry. And you are wonderfully symmetric! That's why, regardless of what you're wearing, I am in trouble when I am around you. In fact, you were much sexier when I saw you ... naked and clothless ... in my imagination!" he replied.

David's head would have surely exploded with unbearable lust had he seen how alluring Roxye felt upon hearing his voice at the other end of the line! With a fire ignited in her mind, Roxye found herself struggling to select an outfit for the soiree. Naturally, she was more critical of herself than necessary, a common side effect experienced by those newly in love. Agreeing to reconvene, they ended the call, allowing Roxye to delve back into her wardrobe in search of the perfect attire. Finally deciding, Roxye opted for her red plunging neck bell sleeves dress, chosen with David in mind. On her, the dress's color would serve as a fitting reflection of the simmering feelings and emotions—passion, sexuality, love, and joy—that had filled her heart since her arrival on the island.

By around 6 PM, Roxye was impeccably dressed from head to toe, leaving nothing to chance in her preparation. As the final touch in her seductive ensemble, she selected her Tom Ford Santal Blush perfume for the soirée. This fragrance exudes femininity with its musky and sandalwood undertones. Described by Tom Ford as a "textured fusion of creamy sandalwood and exotic eastern spices colliding with sumptuous woods and florals," Santal Blush offered a soft, naked glamor with a mysterious allure.

Meanwhile, Clarissa had meticulously arranged everything to entertain her guests, particularly her daughter's special guest. Seated in the living room, the besotted lady anxiously attended to every detail of her front entrance, pacing herself in anticipation and imagining it as a spectacle for David's senses.

The speed of time seems to synchronize with the pacing of our lives. So Roxye kept seeing the exact same time on the watch no matter how many times she impulsively checked it out. As if for the enamored lady, the time has stopped since her lover isn't yet in the house! But right after she made a quick trip to the lady's room, David was at the front door! Once Clarissa had settled him in the family room, she hurried to quell her daughter's anxious anticipation behind the door. Time seemed to stretch on endlessly as she rushed through her facial touch-up. But as Roxye approached her beloved, his blissful demeanor reassured her that her expectations were indeed being realized in his mind. "Welcome, my love! It's truly special to have you here!" she exclaimed as they embraced each other. She wanted to keep hugging him for as long as she had been waiting for him, and David, for his part, wanted to hold her as tight as he had desired her!

"Darling, you're absolutely breathtaking! Your perfume... Aaaaah! If only I could hold you forever!" exclaimed David, utterly captivated, as he whispered into Roxie's ear.

"Let's all sit down at the dinner table, shall we?" proposed a slightly exasperated Clarissa, seeing how tightly her potential son-in-law held her daughter.

That seemed to snap both David and Roxye out into reality! So, hand in hand, they ultimately moved in the direction of the dinner room. So far, despite David's lateness, he was the evening's first guest. About half of the invitees randomly arrived past seven in the evening and then were escorted to rejoin the pair at the table. Many flattering comments were directed at Clarissa's daughter about how fabulous she looked in that red outfit or how great the duo looked together. All that talking finally made holes in their stomachs, especially Roxie's, who, since the night before, intentionally had been "starving" herself to be able to fit into her dress. As Roxye suggested, her mother finally nodded to her two kitchen ladies' helpers to start serving dinner.

Some people yearn for what they lack in life, and the moment strangely intensified Roxye's longing. While she was captivated by David's enchantment with her feminine allure at that moment, she couldn't help but wonder, "What happens after tonight?" This question consumed her thoughts as the beautiful evening began to fade. The mere contemplation of it stirred a sudden tension deep within her. To distract herself, she swiftly excused herself from the dining room. Post-Barbados, she craved something more fulfilling than the emotional void that had resided in her heart before this trip.

"I am sorry, love. But life isn't fair. I have been by myself all my life. And I am tired of being alone fending for myself all along," Roxye poured out her heart to her boyfriend after he rejoined her in the backyard.

"I know! Regardless of how lovely it is, tonight isn't gonna be enough. Same here; I don't know what I'm gonna do when you leave. Fortunately, we are no longer kids. We will talk tomorrow to devise a plan to correct such unfairness. Come here!" David sympathetically said before taking her into his comforting arms.

"I love you. Thanks for your understanding. It seems that I needed you in my life more than 1 even realized. I hope that I didn't make a scene there. We better return inside before my folks start...," she finally suggested.

David and Roxye returned to a quasi-sleepy room. Although it was getting late, one could suspect that the heavy meal was exacting its toll too on them. Some guests have already gone home. Other siblings remained a little longer for a proper goodbye, knowing that Roxye would return to the US the day after tomorrow. As for Clarissa, she returned to the kitchen to assist in rearranging the kitchen's wares and materials. Her daughter, again alone, was finalizing with her boyfriend the agenda and itinerary for their last day together before flying back home. After he left, Roxye went back inside the house to join her mother for a complete debriefing of the soiree and their guests.

Chapter 20
Securing a "Husband for the Lord!"

In the morning, as Roxye gazed forward, she found herself in a state akin to that of a first-time expectant mother, apprehensive of the labor pains yet fully aware of their inevitability if she is to embrace the profound joy of motherhood. Firmly rooted in her belief that unmarried life for a woman equates to tragedy, Roxye remains resolute, undeterred by the prospect of biological discomfort or the constraints of rigid religious doctrine. With Bridgetown's Boardwalk trail as their chosen destination, Roxye and her partner embark on a journey fraught with significance. For her, the stakes are undeniably high—it is time to fulfill her life's purpose, a notion frequently reiterated by her siblings. Moreover, she seeks to discover the elusive missing piece that will ensure her emotional well-being and preserve her perceived 'sanity.' Above all, Roxye is acutely aware of her spiritual standing before the divine, feeling the weight of her commitment to maintain her chastity, threatened by the relentless pull of her own desires. As each moment passes without proper preparation, Roxye senses the gravity of the day ahead, recognizing its pivotal nature in shaping her future.

Roxye was impatiently waiting to be picked up by her boyfriend. For the first time ever this week, David managed to arrive on time for any *rendezvous* because he didn't want to spare even a minute of their limited time together. I was so relieved that Roxye jumped on him as if they hadn't seen each other for ages! Off they went for Bridgetown's Boardwalk, where they had the discussion that would change their life for good. They had no chaperones since it was their last day before flying home. "If I would ever get a chance to antenuptial tropicalize her southern region, it would be today..." David reasoned in himself.

"Boardwalk, according to a tourist's website, is about one mile of track running along Hastings Rocks. It links a string of beautiful beaches." Above all, it's a pleasant area for a long stroll, giving them both a beautiful setting and enough time to iron out the proper ground rules, to set up the "logistics" of their soon-to-be long-distance romantic relationship, and, above all, to agree on a specific timeframe for el nozze. Once there, they took full advantage of such an enchanting setting. They talked through it all. She heard the answers that she never wanted to hear. He was happy that she felt pleased with his reassurances and promises. So by early afternoon, Roxye's way ahead became clearer. How does a woman show gratitude to her man?

The prospect of leaving David behind and her own inflamed sexual desire have challenged both Roxye's perspective and surely made her uncomfortable around him. She fell into a hyper-mating state that happened to coincide with David's crushing rut ever since she landed. Will Protestantism rescue her from herself? Even Roxye had her own doubts..1!

By mid-morning, Roxye was already on her way to the airport. Clarissa, John, Julia, and David rode with her in the car. "Roye, when did you get home last night? We tried to call you, but we couldn't get a hold of you," her mother asked with a slight frustration in her tone. Not only did she not see her daughter the night before, but Roxye also failed to talk with her in the morning, ostensibly for lack of time. So she reasoned this was her last chance! So, albeit in public! Discerning how loaded Clarissa's question was, John and his girl would rather be anywhere else but in the car. David didn't feel any better! So he feigned checking the latest news on his cell phone! As for the intended party, she wished she was alone with her man thirty-five thousand feet high, above the sea, because there was no good response to her mom's public inquiry!

If done artfully, trying to change the subject was Roxye's only viable option. So she pulled a beautiful pair of earrings from her handbag and handed them to her mother. " Oh! I almost forgot to give them to you. Aren't they pretty, mom? They should look good on you!" she said with a hybrid look on her face as she was putting on her mother's ears. Her quick stunt seemed to work magic! Clarissa's appreciative smile obliterated her initial concerns about her daughter's trumped-up morality! And it also changed the tense atmosphere inside the car, too. It was already too late when she wanted to have a second swing at her. John pulled into the airport passenger terminal. Then the 'suspected' couple smiled in real relief!

Roxye's baggage on the sidewalk all stepped forward to their respective final goodbye. Finally, it was her boyfriend's turn. With mixed emotions on his face, David slowly moved forward to embrace his departing girl.

"Love, I know! I know! It's really hard for me, too. As you know, it's in our mutual interest that I leave you for now," Roxye said to his ears, comforting him while her folks were waiting for him in the car. "Thanks for giving us another chance. I really enjoyed every minute with you, especially … the ones that we blissfully shared after Boardwalk's stroll …!" He said cryptically and almost with a hushed voice, being mindful that Roxye's folks were at a mere earshot distance away in the car. "Oh! Those….! Maybe we presumptuously enjoyed "it," but at least I feel the Lord wants us to be together." Her delayed religious conscience then tried to invent some moral justification for whatever they'd done yesterday afternoon.

However, in the middle of those endless goodbyes, a pissed-off cabbie blasted his horn for John to move out of his way. His passengers were running late for their flight! It rattled the emotional couple. "Everybody's patience ran out. I better go before missing my flight! My love, come here again! I love you so much!" Roxye continued as she tightly hugged and kissed her man before entering the airport lobby for good.

Roxye was an emotional mess on the plane because her trip was a resounding success! On the one hand, she came for David; he was easy picking like low-lying, ripped, alluring, delicious fruits! She also had an enchanted vacation with the man of her dreams on a paradisiac island. They are committed to each other; they want more of the same. In sum, in so many ways, he gave her way more than she bargained for! Even her family unexpectedly showered her with love.

On the other hand, though, alone again, her thoughts and flying back to the same big American void after such a week gave her some emotional wallops. She felt as she did before her vacation trip. She felt awkward about how easily and eagerly she gave herself to David after just a few days, although she enjoyed every bit of it then. She was momentarily confused about why she had to leave behind the man who made her feel so happy. However, she realized a significant change in her thought pattern. She had choices. Besides old mental treks leading up to the old sadness, loneliness, and feelings of failure, she also had fresh trails of positive memories and experiences with her boyfriend to veer on instead during this moment. What a relief for her…!

"… Where are we going after leaving here, love?"

"I have a friend, Stanley, who happens to live not too far from here. I have been telling him about you. He surely wanted to meet you unless you wanna go home."

"Nah! I'm all yours today. Anywhere with you but home, as of yet!"

"Like you read my mind. Then let's get out of here… to see him."

"I can feel some… tension in your hand! Is Stanley really waiting for us? And, how far isn't too far, Hon?" Roxye sheepishly asked.

"Ten or maybe fifteen minutes away. Don't you worry! He told me where to find the key if he had gone to work. Nothing bad will happen to you!" David mysteriously replied.

"So shouldn't we just call Stanley to confirm before heading there, then?… Unless we aren't talking about the same thing, are we, love?" his girlfriend said, gauging his real intentions.

"Sweetie pie, whatever you're thinking about, that's exactly what we are talking about, just so you know!" he stated, staying strategically opaque.

"Then should I be worried? Because your demeanor is the same as when you were in your backyard the first night that we met there!" Roxye finally verbally expressed her suspicion.

"Why should you, love? However, it's encouraging that you remembered that. Nothing has changed, indeed. To the contrary! I don't know what to make of the fact that now you're putting even more stuff into my head!" David acknowledged her complicity but with a poker swag.

"What do I do now, love? You don't need any help from me. It seems your mind has been filled with whatever is making you feel the way you have been feeling alone! For now, please keep your eyes on the road and your hand off of me! For you've been staring at me with a ravishing look since the very night I set foot on this island!" she indeed hit the bullseye!

"Look! Here is Stanley's building! It's a chic neighborhood, isn't it, babe?" as he pointed his finger toward a building on the left-hand side.

"It looks nice! Do you see his car, though? What is this sound?" an unsuspected Roxye took the bait readily set by her 'hungry man.'

"There was a work emergency. Unfortunately, I won't be home until after midnight! So make yourself home. I will see your girlfriend another time!" It's a text message from Stanley." David nonchalantly announced to her as he extended his hand to prove it on his phone's screen.

Roxye's heart pounded as she realized there was no escape. She knew deep down what her boyfriend, David, wanted from her. His persistent advances and her own longing for security had worn down her resolve. Now, standing at the front door of David's friend's house, she couldn't deny the truth any longer.

She had been avoiding facing the inevitable, clinging to the hope that the road ahead would stretch on endlessly. But here she was, confronted with the reality of David's desires and her own wavering willpower. Had her longing for love blinded her to her own principles?

Roxye failed to be honest with herself on that occasion. Maybe, initially she was sincere, She wanted to do things the correct way, God's way. But it was just wishful thinking without a sensible plan of action and proper guardrails to herself temporary lapse of judgment. Our heart is erratic even under the best circumstances. And one in love tends to be worse. So a person under its spell needs to be very careful not to put too much credence to its incitements. For doing so, a person would end up crashing on the primrose path. What about the gentlemen?

He couldn't help but think only about himself. People are supposed to be together to help each other out. To help each other to become a better version of themselves. Unfortunately, David was thinking about the wrong things all along. He wanted to mark his territory so to speak. He minimized the strength and depth of Roxye's love for him. He failed to be patient at a critical time in their burgeoning relationship. May that was the first crack at the basis of it, either they realized or not then. Now, high up on the air, in a contemplative moment, Roxye has been vividly reliving the climactic events of the night before when they arrived at Stanley's empty apartment…

"Mom!, would you like something to drink?" the flight attendant dared ask Roxye, completely unaware that she was stepping in her passenger's dream…

"Please go away! Stanley isn't home right now! We're …busy…!"

Her ill-timed question elicited a mysterious answer from the cowgirl while breaking both the barrier between dream and reality and her momentum in that spatial position…

As expected, Roxye's absurd and insolent reply baffled the flight attendant and drew the attention of some nearby passengers. So, to diffuse such unwanted attention, she quickly apologized to the lady and, this time, logically answered her initial question. "A ginger ale with some ice, please!" As she turned to fetch her drink, Roxye smiled. Relieved knowing that no one would ever know what her day-residue dream was all about while hoping none of them would ever think that she was nuts either! So she buried her head in a book as a pretense until the plane finally landed a few hours later.

Chapter 21
The Storm Made By Immigration

Carlexa and her sister Chesty were scanning the faces of people coming out of the airport's lobby. "Look! There she is!" Chesty suddenly proclaimed on seeing her big sister's moving silhouette. So they both ran to welcome their sister! "We've missed you!" they said almost in unison. "But your sublime look tells us it wasn't the case for you! Isn't that true? Carlexa quickly asked. "Believe me, I am as fatigued as you are eager to hear it all! However, I won't dare to expect you to stop nagging me until...! So I could call my boyfriend when I get home, girls; what would you like to know?"

"First of all, you misled us into believing you flew back home to visit your mom, right?" said Carlexa and Chesty, who had waited almost a week to ask her that question face to face.

Absolutely, I swear! I never meant to cause any trouble! It was just a trip idea full of uncertainties. So, it wouldn't make sense for me to have been more precise beforehand, right? I mean, I had to actually be there to understand everything. You both knew I wasn't exactly thrilled about being here alone without a partner." Roxye stated matter-of-factly.

"You could have said that. Don't you think we could have understood you?" They said with a bit of frustration.

Probably! But I wouldn't have any viable answers for your next volley of questions, though!" said Roxye, trying to tap into their understanding.

"OK! Then! You are being forgiven! But do you have better answers for us now, after this trip?" they conceded.

"Absolutely! David was like an open book waiting to be read! That's why I'm so happy I took the chance to visit him. It seems everything fell into place perfectly! He was quick to agree, reigniting our romance, which made me incredibly happy! So, we spent a wonderful week together filled with engaging talks and fun activities, all in a beautiful island setting. And on top of that, I returned home with a solid plan to tie the knot... Isn't this everything we've ever hoped for?" Roxy exclaimed. "Whoa! You drop on us a boatload of information here! Let's try to unpack some of them here and right now! What do you mean… by "stress-releasing activities"? Did you have…? Did he uncork your holy grail..?" Both Carlexa and Chesty wanted to know.

"What's your question.? Did I have what right now.? You asked me if David and I go biblical? How do you expect me to answer that? What should I tell you?" she rhetorically asked.

"What about just the simple truth since you have heard us so well!" they both said in unison.

"I needed to feel that I was desired, appreciated, and loved!" Roxye finally confessed.

"Mmmm! It sounds like my sister has gotten her groove back! Is that why you want to marry him now?"

"That and for all the reasons in the world!" she answered convincingly.

"Except that David isn't a churchgoer like you, is he? Does that give you any pause, sis? We can understand that he wants to devour your fetching body. Who wouldn't? But should you make such a big decision? Unless you are like some religious women who believe that the alley between their two Greek columns is the surest and shortest shortcut to secure a future husband… for God! But who are we to judge? How useful would a modern maiden girl be to the Lord?" they finally acquiesced.

However, amidst their banter, they couldn't shake the concern about the differing beliefs between Roxye and David. While Roxye found solace and guidance in her faith, David's path seemed to diverge from the church's teachings. It was a point of contention that lingered in the air, casting a shadow over Roxye's decision to marry him. Yet, despite their reservations, they ultimately yielded to Roxye's conviction, recognizing that love often defies rationality.

"Thank you, girls, for your feminine understanding! I love you so much!" Roxye said with relief in her heart.

Although she appreciated having her supportive sisters around, Roxye was relieved when they finally arrived home from the airport. She could finally escape their relentless questioning and retreat to her room for some peace and quiet. Roxye knew she needed to preserve her sanity because, in the upcoming months, she would be navigating a long-distance relationship, dealing with US immigration issues, and preparing for a sudden wedding, all while juggling a full-time job. That's modern love for you!

Late into the evening, Roxye finally found a moment to call David before bed, as they had planned. Their relationship had taken on a new seriousness, and they made sure to have a brief but meaningful conversation in anticipation of their upcoming reunion somewhere in the Caribbean Sea.

"My love! How are you doing? I've missed you so much already! How was your flight?" David eagerly exclaimed as he heard Roxye's voice on the other end of the line.

"Missing isn't the correct word! I am not sure yet how long I will try to survive sanely in this big social wilderness without you being here at my side! Ah, that! My 'ride home' was unexpectedly titillating, to say the least!" she mysteriously replied.

"You meant...your flight..my love?

"Yeah! If you will!" she said, unwilling to provide any helpful context.

"But, since you left, the island morphed from an oasis into an unbearable inferno! Leaving here without isn't the same! When is your appointment with the lawyer again?" he concurred.

"Alan appreciates how urgent our case is. His office has already prepared all the paperwork. I will stop there in his office just to sign them up after work tomorrow. Imagine this: you could be here, next to me in twelve months' time, and then, within three, be my wedded husband at once but for life!" she said excitedly.

"The process of getting married is messy, indeed. I guess getting a woman as good as you couldn't come easy, isn't it? So, in the meantime, I will try to focus on loving you more intensely and keeping my eyes on the prize..! All of that should kill off the time pretty fast, don't you think, sweetie pie?" David promised rhetorically if that was even possible.

"Getting married sure is a messy business. Finding a gem like you would never be easy. Right? So, while we wait, I'll focus on loving you more and keeping my eye on the prize..! That should make time fly, don't you think, sweetie pie?" David pledged, half in jest, if that were even possible.

Within a year, their daily routine spanning across the ocean, the anticipation of marriage, and many texts, video chats, and calls sustained David and Roxye's blossoming romance despite their initial fear of failure. Their love was still young and inexperienced in every aspect. Being in a long-distance relationship meant facing temptations from different cultures and lifestyles. They believed overcoming these obstacles would only strengthen their bond when they finally exchanged vows. Roxye even half-jokingly thought that her last passionate act must have left a lasting impression on David, ensuring his fidelity.

Meanwhile, David hoped he had proven himself to be a reliable partner, both tamed and spirited when needed. These self-assured beliefs became their lifelines as they navigated the challenges of their relationship. And before long, David's visa was approved. Now, the question remained: where would David stay once he arrived? They finally opted to rent a friend's basement apartment until the wedding.

The hustle and bustle of preparing for marriage consumed Roxie and her friends more than anything else. She had a husband-to-be waiting for her, and the pressure was on! Time was of the essence because the immigration clock was ticking away. They had to tie the knot within three months to meet the legal requirement for his visa.

First things first, they had to wrap up the alterations on the wedding gown. Then, there was the task of finding an affordable venue for the marriage celebrations, including all the bridal showers and other related events. On top of that, they needed to scout out a picturesque park nearby for some memorable photos. And let's not forget the never-ending task of finalizing the guest list.

We don't know how Roxye pulled it off, but they got married as planned! "Marriage is hard, even ...under the best circumstances!' But then, that was a Martian thought for the new couple. For David, it's harvesting season, after all! They have a place to go! So after their Hawaiian honeymoon, Roxye returned home ravaged, weakened, visibly happy... and pregnant!" No surprise there! Because, after all this closed-up, churchgoing woman turned out to be a sexual dynamo! And, as expected, David freaking loved it! Who wouldn't? The lady of the house was relieved to settle down finally. "Gone were my old frequent migraines!," she confided in one of her girlfriends. The only outstanding matter to figure out was David's professional transition.

Roxye returned to work while David stayed home, religiously waiting for her woman wife. That situation lasted for many months. At first, it fit both parties well; She had a valet husband ready to fire up her engine at peak performance on command. As for David, he kept asking himself why not to love. In this world, no good thing lasts forever! Eventually, through a good friend of his wife finally got him enrolled in an electricity apprenticeship program. For understandable reasons, the man of the house wasn't initially thrilled about leaving the newlywed's nest but was keenly aware that having a decent job was his primary way to regain some of his husband's privileges and responsibilities.

For years, David has been on a journey to redefine his role in their relationship beyond being merely his wife's trophy man. The thrill of their early days together gradually faded, exposing the harsh reality that it's incredibly challenging for an adult beginner to carve out a successful path in the US job market. Roxye, with her keen insight, understood the complexities of their situation from the start. She firmly believed in the adage, "The end justifies the means!" Remarkably, she has shown no sign of impatience, either then or now. Her wisdom told her that patience was essential, as it would take time before she could relinquish her role as the primary provider in the household.

This journey has been a learning curve for David, filled with introspection and determination to contribute more significantly. He has been exploring various avenues to find his footing and add value in ways he hadn't imagined before. Meanwhile, Roxy's steadfast support and understanding have been the cornerstone of their evolving partnership. Together, they are navigating this phase of their lives with resilience, hope for the future, and the fulfillment of their shared dreams and aspirations.

In the problematic American matrimonial landscape, Roxye realized long ago that she would have to sing for her super, to find a decent and responsible man. So she didn't mind it at all! It was wise to put her new "gifted horse" to good use. "*Noli equi dentes inspicere Donati*," she kept reminding herself, especially when things were going so well for the family. First of all, she is married, at last! She has an effective "standing prescription" for the bouts of episodic migraine with detestable side effects. Also, thanks to David, she removed her family's and Barjan society's stigma associated with her previous marital status. So she threw it away as one does to the trash at the first opportunity! Finally, since she was with her second child, her birth would eventually remove any doubt about her womanhood. Those were exciting times for the Clarke's, indeed.

Mrs. Clarke's life seemed to be ticking off boxes on Maslow's Hierarchy of Needs checklist with the arrival of her second child and her flourishing career. But lurking beneath this facade of contentment was a danger zone waiting to be navigated. Why? Because her initial concerns about her husband David losing interest in her due to post-pregnancy weight gain proved to be unfounded. In fact, David not only accepted but embraced her newfound curves, expressing to a friend that he was somewhat addicted to them!

On the professional front, Mrs. Clarke soared up the corporate ladder with multiple promotions, each bringing more responsibilities, higher pay, and increased prestige. Yet, amidst this climb, she began to notice a disconnect in her marriage. Like the ever-flowing river, professionally her husband seemed to have moved to a different stream, leaving her feeling adrift.

David started to realize that Roxye, his wife, was undergoing a transformation of her own. As she ascended the ranks in her career, her persona evolved, leaving him struggling to keep pace with the changes.

David's strengths have definitely become his weaknesses in Roxye's new circle of friends. He is a licensed electrician but a tradesman nonetheless, not a white-collar husband working in one of the town's corporate skyscrapers. Also, although he is bringing in good money, he has to go through the basement's door and bathe himself before she can kiss or hug him after work. Coming to the US from an English-speaking Caribbean country has made it easier to transition, but now his non-British foreign accent makes her uncomfortable, annoyingly answering her friends' questions about it anytime he opens his mouth. Further, Roxye used to like the fact that her husband too is a sexual dynamo who likes to ravage her, leaving her weak, gasping for breath ... and pregnant a few times. But now she complains that David rides her wild and he is too rugged for her liking! And she is too busy and tired for that! Because of her last promotion, not only does she regularly work after hours, but also she comes back home to work!

Clarke's marriage was at an inflection point. It seems that it's falling apart from its success! In hindsight, though, they should have anticipated how hard it would be for those two incongruent childhoods to merge into a sustainable marital environment. But none of them was willing to put forth the required efforts! Unfortunately, they couldn't see anything bigger than themselves since they were self-absorbed! Friends can sense and see something is not quite right with them after a while. Family relatives were finally aware of their problems, too. They knew that It was unraveling. David forever wanted more of the same from his wife. Roxye, for her part, no longer wanted what her husband was bringing to the table. She finds him no longer worthy of who she has become and what she now brings to the table. Thus, the entire Clarke family is falling. It causes much pain and misery for the whole family. But that's exactly what Roxie wants now! So they both accepted that fact. The only real question was if softening the blows remains a possibility, for, after all, who prepared for crash landing?

Chapter 22
To Hunker Down In "The Cushions of The Sea"

For the time being, women will continue to captivate men with their enchanting femininity. They will keep adapting themselves to fit into different roles, sometimes appearing as mysterious as the night yet as enchanting as a rose in bloom. They may even go to great lengths, even swearing under oath if necessary, to secure the closest spot when the calls come. Yet, men often struggle to understand a simple truth: that a woman remains a woman, regardless of her artfulness or physical appearance. Until this realization dawns upon them, they will persist in viewing women as fertile grounds for their desires, much like hungry farmers sowing seeds in a field.

Even men, whether married or enjoying plenty of attention, find themselves torn between reason and desire. Their minds sway more often towards the latter, despite their best intentions. Once a woman finds her way into a man's heart, she becomes a permanent fixture, impossible to remove even with the most advanced medical treatments. This phenomenon, known as "the other woman syndrome," defies logic and scientific explanation, rooted deeply in the inexplicable realm of romantic love.

Despite the illogical nature of eros love, some partners have attempted to shield their loved ones from falling victim to its spell.

"We strive to remain good friends and support each other," an experienced African wife once told me. The entire house is "the bed," she continued, emphasizing the importance of closeness and intimacy within a relationship. "When the southern region becomes tropical, nobody has time for formalities!" she added, highlighting the need for spontaneity and passion.

Another friend shared her perspective, explaining that for women with intelligence and emotional maturity, understanding that any space can become a "bed" when shared with their partner. They aim to maintain a strong connection and protect their relationship from external threats by adapting to their man's preferences and desires, vice versa.

These women and men see themselves as the guardians of their marriage bed, actively working to keep the spark alive and fend off potential rivals. They understand that physical attraction alone is not enough; availability and commitment are equally crucial.

Ultimately, their mindset revolves around ensuring that their partners remain satisfied and fulfilled, both emotionally and physically. For them, being the ideal partner means being present and attentive, regardless of external distractions or temptations.

Marriage inevitably changes people. The nature, depth, and timing of such changes is anybody's guess. So managing their and marriage partners' concerns requires profound emotional and mental powers that are so lacking in today's society. So folks are marrying and then recanting their heartfelt vows in the same manner, without thinking about tomorrow! And, in the process, they're creating the next generation of broken souls who themselves would continue the same cycle. They are unhappy for lacking what they ever strive for in life and then becoming miserable once they acquire it until they finally trash it in a New York minute! So, our inability to fully enjoy what we possess would be the cause of our undoing.

So, we got back to square one. What do women want to be, once and for all, satisfied? To be more specific, what does a married woman want? Indeed, what would make her truly happy? Could it be a perfect husband, or being perfect herself may do it? Or would motherhood be it? Is it to finally be in peace with the Almighty? She would have run for her life, away from so-called "Higher Knowledge?" Reach for a godlike statute? To be powerful, materially comfortable? To be "*Bien Baisée*" or to be sincerely loved by her man? Unfortunately, even today, the jury is still out!

You don't know what you don't know. Granted, you may have heard of all kinds of stories about marriages. You may also interact with married folks daily or even live under the same roof with some, like your parents, for example. But if you never exchanged the vows, you can never experience what it feels like to be married. A marriage is a truly unique relationship. It exerts tremendous pressure on every square of your soul, hard-pressed every fiber of one's character. Sad to say that many do not survive it! Like in the case of the Titan submersible, the society has been collecting pieces as a result of its catastrophic implosion. Maybe that's one of the reasons the ladies came up with these rules to alleviate the pressure. Maybe! But Do they work? Do they boost your confidence to hitch yourself to the marriage bandwagon? Or have you been, or are you still on the fence?

Chapter 23
A Man's Dilemma

Edwards, a wealthy widow, had one beloved son named Richards, who was a long-time slave. After his death, his vast estates shall be divided between these two. So, on his deathbed, Edwards asked the former to go ahead and select all he ever needs or wants from it. And the latter would then inherit whatever that the son left out. The son thought for a moment and then replied: "Father, please give me the slave! That would be enough for me." Richards rightly reasoned that by becoming the slave's master, he would own all his father had ever possessed after his passing. Thus squashing any basis for personal regret and also avoiding any future acrimony or bad blood with the slave in the process. Richards has killed two birds with just one stone. His approach was practical. Right?

Now, let's dig a bit deeper into Richards' decision and its implications. By choosing to inherit the slave, Richards secured ownership of his father's possessions and demonstrated a keen understanding of human relationships and the dynamics of inheritance.

Richards' decision can be seen as a strategic move, ensuring his comfort and stability while maintaining a harmonious relationship with the slave. Rather than risking potential conflict over the division of his father's estate, Richards opted for a solution that guaranteed both material wealth and interpersonal peace.

Furthermore, Richards' choice reflects his practical mindset and resourcefulness. Instead of being swayed by the allure of wealth and property, he focused on what he deemed most valuable: a harmonious existence free from resentment and discord.

In essence, Richards' decision was not only practical but also enlightened. It exemplifies his ability to navigate complex social dynamics with wisdom and foresight, ensuring both his own well-being and the preservation of amicable relationships within his family.

Ideally, desire should be subordinate to reason. While it's rarely the case, any man who decides to give up his freedom in exchange for a woman must ask some hard bidirectional questions. First, he should ask himself: "Who (type of person) or what (feminine things) are you looking for?" and then, afterward: "Who are you or what are you bringing to the table as a potential 'partner?' We know that thinking and knowing can be painful. But it's good, necessary pain! Therefore, such questions require more than mental suppositions or cosmetic answers. Any false pretense of some kind of 'future mystic power' to change your partner will not do, either. But why does logic seem doomed to play catch up with fleshly desire?

The odds are stacked against a man in his quest for a compatible mate. Like a compass that points northward, a man is automatically hooked up to a woman's face, bosoms, and great divide. These are the enduring elements of his timeless trinity. There is no Christendom without the Trinity dogma; likewise, there is hardly a man who isn't a believer in this quasi-religious, feminine credo. It's the deal breaker! Most of the time, any woman less favored by nature wouldn't have a chance to get that special masculine look unless he is in a challenging situation. But when a man's senses are awakened by a potential lady's physical attractiveness, he would effortlessly credit her with all the good qualities of the world! Then her physical triune trumps all else; at least, until she breaks his fever. Meanwhile, his whole being is certainly laser-focused on the price, no question about it!

A desired bounda is seemingly inescapable. It's like being sucked up in the eye of a strong tornado. If you luckily survived it, then you would never be the same. But exactly what kind of power are we talking about here? You'll be the judge. Imagine a prince who fell in love with his virgin, stunningly beautiful half-sister! As soon as she became aware of his lust for her, she let him know that she was agreeable to becoming his wedded wife, which, back then, was culturally and legally acceptable. However, he wouldn't have any of it! He was locked and loaded! So like a brute beast, he trapped her and forcibly raped her own little, virgin half sister who wanted to help him! "You can't "resist" her extremely fetching body, can you? You want it, now, isn't that right?" he kept hearing … in his head days prior. However, a short time later, our enchanted prince was put to death for being dazzled by a pretty overwhelming stuff.

Femininity has real power. Here is another example. Imagine Max, an experienced Seal Six soldier, on a mission in enemy territory. He finally found himself surrounded by enemy soldiers who vowed to kill him plain and simple, whatever the cost. While in this predicament, he was attracted to a local partner, who could be a lifesaver if they could "cause the commune" to fight it out of this dangerous situation. No, he fell in love with Bella, a maiden young woman fetching "Coke curves," to be more precise. Period. Absolutely nothing has been mentioned about her good qualities or her character.

Moreover, she had no experience whatsoever in military warfare! She was a Hebrew Belle, an absolute stunner! That's it! Maybe he wanted her at his side for her tactical mind or her insight into the local terrain. Sadly, she had no such knowledge either, and he couldn't care less! She was an eyeful, and our soldier's eyes, mind, and heart were full of her, even in this critical situation. What in the world is he going to do? It should clearly call the central command for immediate backup, right?

What our brave soldier did next, and why stunned the military world! He willingly stripped off his special-purpose weaponry, equipment, and special uniform and threw them all in a dumpster. He did exactly what his Belissima had instructed him to. "You will be safe in my warm and loving arms. Oh, Babe! Screw your commander! No need to call them for backup! All the back you ever want to be up is mine! It's all yours forever." Finally, under her debilitating charm, he gave her all his military secure communication devices, which she immediately dropped off in the toilet with a lustful smile. He desired, loved, wanted that body so much that he willingly trashed his training, his freedom, his family, and his country and carelessly put his life in greater danger for you know what!

Later, Bella turned out to be the enemy's mole. So she discreetly summoned her handlers, who, at once, came and captured her unsuspecting, defenseless Romero. They bored his eyes out, put his soul in chains, and kept him in a high-security prison. They were jubilant, so they threw a grandiose national celebration to honor their god, whom they thought had given their country such a great victory. These bonds slowly but surely squeezed her out of his mind and heart. So it was only then that he regained full control of his sanity. Completely sold out and abandoned by his former enchantress, he finally used his mental power to do some deep thinking. He could "see" and realize the foolishness of his behavior. "Sometimes falling in love is worse than being in jail," he probably learned as he experienced both. However, through its vast electronic surveillance and spy network, his government didn't take long to locate Max and confirm that the enemy was holding him as a POW. But what can he do?

Who among us never, in a moment of weakness, failed to do the right thing or did the regrettable wrong thing? Most men could testify about how puny we are when confronted by desired hips that keep hopping... within our minds. At last, liberated from such feminine duress and alone in a dark, miserable pit, Max had plenty of free time to ponder over his predicament. So he further realized that tapping into his training and reconnecting with his command post were his best chances to get back his freedom, redeem himself, or at least salvage what was left of his reputation.

Max secretly devised an escape plan and was able to reestablish contact with his government through diplomatic channels. However, his captors couldn't decode his cryptic communication, even though they tapped into the phone line, as expected. He wanted revenge for the terrible treatment the enemy inflicted on him and his country at all costs. A Pentagon official briefed about Max's game plan later described it as a kamikaze scheme. "The Pentagon" would secretly provide him with all he needed, and he would be willing to give all he had, literally his life, for the cause. And they did. As a result, in his final act, Max killed many more enemy soldiers than he ever did during his entire military career! Max was a classic victim of retroactive interference. Bella's bounda fatally impaired his judgment. So, Max voluntarily chose the primrose path!

Richard's approach, as we investigate deeper into it, reveals a profound consideration for the future. If he had hastily sorted through the estates without careful thought, there's a distinct possibility he would have found himself plagued by regret down the line. After all, a man's perspective on life, desires, and necessities often evolves with time. By opting for his father's slave, Richard potentially spared himself from future anguish. This decision ensured that he wouldn't have to grapple with the weight of choosing incorrectly. Contrastingly, imagine the plight of someone who hastily selects a partner based solely on physical attraction. In moments of difficulty, such a bounda could feel like an unbearable burden to bear. It's a stark reminder of the importance of foresight and deliberation in decision-making, especially when it comes to matters as significant as these.

A complicated man should marry more than a bounda. For, quite often, "pure beauty brings pure pain and nothing less!" Even though any woman won't be able to give you more than what she has, it's always a bad idea to marry for just a physique— however fetching it might be. They often ended up being just deadweight. Such spouses let their emotions color over their views of family matters and other folks and are prone to self-destructive thought patterns and behaviors. Still, even their "only asset" tends to become a liability by sheer misuse or mindlessly underusing it. Finally, their partners' romantic and life dreams ended up being pure, disturbing nightmares!

In considering the idea of marrying the right persona versus a bounda or all things physical about a woman, it's essential to delve into what each option entails. Marrying the right persona offers the promise of a fulfilling connection, even if it might not be extravagantly lavish. But you would get to enjoy the whole package: a personality to live for *and* available bounda, albeit au sac! On the other hand, imagine having a banquet of gourmet filet mignon dishes, carefully curated and presented, but behind bulletproof glass! At first glance, it's a tantalizing prospect, but sooner one would realize it was just an attractive mirage! Your move!

Happy would be those who protect their minds and hearts from the glare of physical prettiness! A full access to a banquet of peanut butter sandwiches awaits such ones. It may not sound as luxurious and as appetizing as a promised caviar dish, such unrestricted access to a staple and comforting food will be all one will ever need to survive in the trenches of marital life. For, the choice becomes clearer when considering the frustration of having the sexiest, prettiest, or curviest partner who remains emotionally and sexually distant or unavailable.

Partners prioritizing their appearance often lack the time or inclination to invest in genuine friendships or personal development. They may rely on their looks to navigate life without honing essential qualities like critical thinking or empathy. This self-absorption can lead to a sense of entitlement and a reluctance to alleviate the suffering of others.

In light of these considerations, it becomes evident that marrying a persona, rather than a mere appealing bounda, is the wiser choice. But how does one navigate the complex maze of captivating boundas to find the right persona?

It requires a discerning eye and a willingness to look beyond surface-level qualities. Instead of being swayed by external appearances or societal expectations, focus on finding someone who values connection and authenticity. Look for signs of emotional intelligence, empathy, and a genuine desire to cultivate meaningful relationships.

Engage in deep conversations, observe how they interact with others, and pay attention to their actions over time. Inquire from who has to know about any potential mate. Trust what the facts will be telling you and prioritize qualities that are enduring and meaningful in the long run.

The right persona may not always be immediately apparent in the labyrinth of arresting boundas. It requires patience, introspection, and a willingness to look beyond superficialities. But by prioritizing substance over surface, you can find a partner who enriches your life in ways that transcend mere appearances.

Chapter 24
Selecting a Marriage Partner

"One takes a considerable risk by tying up the knots in matrimony before getting any potential mate checked out by a competent 'vet,'" said a woman with plenty of masculine experience in hindsight. Aside from the joke lies a fundamental truth: It's crucial to properly vet someone before taking them into matrimony. Failure to go through such a vetting process may end up marrying a mirage. For example, soon enough, you might find out that you married someone and later discover that inside an adult's body, mind, and emotions are those of a child! How sad and frustrating to find yourself married to an attractive child!

On the flip side, "If you would marry wisely, marry your *equal*," said a poet. Before going any further, it requires you to take an honest look at none other than yourself. Are you prepared for marriage? What are your strengths and weaknesses? Are you a happy person? Are you a pessimistic or optimistic person? What are you looking for in marriage? Do you have thinking ability, common sense, or discernment? The ability to objectively perform such honest self-appraisal is a good sign of emotional maturity. Thus, in return, you should be able to evaluate any potential mate's emotional level, too.

But even such an emotionally intelligent person isn't guaranteed to select his equal automatically! Why? Physical beauty and sheer sexual attractiveness are like minefields, especially for men, or like Damocles's sword over their heads. For " *Bèl fanm se bèl malè*!" says a Haitian proverb. Also, they tend to cloud men's judgment, impairing their ability to see beyond the initial nuptial nights or envision that thinking ability and emotional maturity are preferred over a pretty face, generous poitrines, and generous derrière for a permanent and happy relationship. And no amount and frequency of "private exercise" will be able to compensate for such profound personal deficiencies. Unfortunately, nearly all men, especially the youths, once dazzled, and often overrated their ability to make up for them.

Even under the best circumstances, marriage is hard! Then imagine how troubled a man would be when he realized, after their honeymoon, that his fiancée has gone missing and won't ever return home! Who will convince him that all his love and attention should be devoted to the "new stranger" living in his place? And would he ever believe that his recent mental and emotional "growth spurts" do not easily negate the fact that an earlier version of him had solemnly promised to "love, honor and cherish her?." Unfortunately, she would be going through the same traumatic changes and then developing the same syndrome! At first, most men and women will internalize such shocks while trying hard to figure out what had happened to them, their love, and their early blissful joy.

"I don't understand what happened to us, but I just don't love Bill anymore. I can't help it. He's not the man I married."

I've outgrown my wife. She can't give me what I need. She doesn't have it and never will. I wish I had seen that before we got married."—The Marriage Gap.

But sooner or later, the end result of such reflections would inevitably lead them to a crossroads. Emotional adulthood would have been helpful there, but the lack of it has brought them so soon to the impasse in the first place! They found themselves pressed between a rock and a hard place! So, will they follow the temptingly easy, popular primrose path? Or will they look deep down in the history of their relationship and come up with a decent reason to stick it together, patiently working hard to go beyond their initial nunchi-type love but going on developing Jeong? Could they find at least one good enough reason…? If not, that would tell all you need to know about how 'marriage material' they were!

Remember, even under the best circumstances, marriage is still the hardest relationship under this Sun! It's crucial to choose a partner with whom you will find plenty of great reasons to happily stay with when, never if, "the tribulations in the flesh" do come. So always marry someone for their personality! Please keep in mind that a potential mate's personality results from many factors such as parental history, childhood, education, circle of friends, or one's life's outlook. So all check them all out before you start humming "Le ça ira!"

Choosing a life partner is like picking the best fruit from a tree. You want something that looks good on the outside and tastes even better on the inside. Like a fruit's sweetness comes from its soil, water, and sun, a person's personality is shaped by various influences.

Think about it like a recipe. Each ingredient contributes to the final flavor. In this case, parental genes add a dash of inherited traits;

childhood experiences sprinkle in memories and habits, education is the main ingredient for knowledge and understanding, friends add a pinch of influence, and life's outlook is the seasoning that brings it all together.

Choosing a partner isn't just about the immediate attraction or the superficial qualities. It's about finding someone whose personality is a complement to yours, someone you can weather life's storms with. So, take your time, observe, and get to know the essence of who they are beyond the surface. Because when you marry for personality, you're laying the foundation for a strong and enduring relationship.

How much do you know about her parents? Would you choose them as your own parents based on what you know? What about her upbringing? Would you raise your own child like that? Would you prefer to have a similar childhood environment? Does she have enough education to know and appreciate the difference between an aspiration, a thought, a feeling, and a fact? Is her mind elastic enough to be able to conversate about random topics without being easily offended?

What is her circle of friends? Are they real folks with good values? Instead, are they primarily virtual or Hollywood friends? How well do you know her friends? Would you choose her best friends for at least your friends on the basis of what you know about them? What about her life's views? Is she willing to give herself, extending herself to others? Or is she mainly buried in herself or her face? Also, is she a realistic person? Is she comfortable in her skin? Also, some women become as heavy as lead once they get married! So would she treat you as her husbandly partner or view and treat you instead as her new wife sitter? Is it how you would like your wife to be after the honeymoon? Or would you prefer her to remain as convenient as a fiancee or a backpack? Will she allow you to make love on the beach and intensely enjoy it as you would? Or in her car or yours? Yes, will she be a liberated enough woman who will use every square foot of the house to enhance her carnal knowledge? You see! Got to find out!

A wise man would try to acquire as much information as possible about the above-mentioned matters before selecting a marriage partner in the labyrinth of the Great Divide. Why? Usually, personalities aren't easily profoundly altered by changing circumstances. Once married, your whole world changes in a New York minute! So steady partners will help each other to weather those changes nicely and continue forward. Also, remember that "cicadas can be happy and rowdy, for they have voiceless wives." If you can blaze just a trail through the feminine triune to select the right persona wisely, you will undoubtedly end up with the best of both worlds! Jumping off in matrimony with a matching personality will definitely and considerably soften the marital blows!

Chapter 25
How To Anchor Your Man

HUSBAND WANTED—Seeking a loving, marriage-minded man, even-tempered, good provider, age 27-40; please send a photo. Sincere and lonely. Want Ad #312456

We feel for anyone, man or woman, who is experiencing such a frustrating situation. If you are now married, and you can sympathize with such people, right? But remember that lots of people have been married but are now either separated, divorced, or worse, killed by the very person who swore to love and cherish them until death do them apart! What's the point? You see, being married happens to be just an opportunity! What would you make of yours? There are all kinds of dangers that are lurking around your family, old ones and new ones! Unfortunately, the biggest threat to your sacred relationship is ... you yourself! That's why this old Hebrew proverb states:

"The truly wise woman or man builds up her house, but the foolish one tears it down with her own hands."

How powerful! Conscientious partners must remember that their living place isn't a court with endless arguments or an arena where fights keep happening for senseless reasons. "Learn when to shut up," said the guy who has been married for 75 years. He is right but what he said isn't. Another old Hebrew proverb even said more beautifully almost five thousand years ago: "Beginning a fight is like opening a floodgate; Before the quarrel breaks, take your leave." "It takes two to make an argument. If one shuts up, the other eventually will stop.," the elderly husband finally explained. So, when your husband stops, please don't interpret his silence as an insult or as if he is carelessly ignoring your feelings! So strive to make your house a haven of peace and tranquility where love and kindness flourish. No one in their right mind would intentionally destroy their familial house. However, it keeps happening! "Why?" you may wonder. "As humans, we [tend to] replicate the same dysfunction within our original family structure with our relationships and partnerships until we do the healing work." Life, 1 swear.

And plenty of women out there are real 'balls eaters'! With their great divide, they would swallow up your puny men whole in a split second without a hint of remorse! Similarly, like heat-seeking missiles, most men, after all, aren't too concerned about decor, shape, or marital status, for they're ultimately looking for fresh… 'milk,' not ownership. Period. So don't let your behavior distract your partner from its source. Human sexuality is governed by timing, geography, and availability. So married partners must avoid developing the mistaken 'we're married, he's good' attitude. For emotionally or sexually depleted partners, foster a foreplay environment for infidelity. Still, everyone must be mindful of another insidious but potent threat.

On a job site in Maryland, I met a mild-tempered guy named Madsen from Pennsylvania, another US state.

"I don't have a life!" he replied flatly with a frustrated face when I asked him how he was doing that morning.

Taking a back at his frank but grave assessment, my curiosity peaked. I continued by inquiring about the reason(s) why of such a grim reckoning.

"Home," he continued, "is becoming more and more unbearable with my wife's never-ending 'honey's to-do list. And always laser-focused on my flaws or what I failed to do in the past! She hardly expresses or shows any appreciation for what I have done. I am getting bloody tired of it. She made my life miserable, having the impression that she saw me just as her errant boy. Honesty, for a while, I feel truly "liberated" when I am at work, away from home!"

"Oh! My … Madsen, it must be tough for you! I said to sympathize a little.

"Indeed, it is! Heaven knows that I stay put so far mainly because it's just cheaper to keep her!" he finally lashed out.

I never forgot both his face and how overwhelmed Madsen was. I have been wondering which marriage partner would like to cause so much pain to her mate. Statistically, a lot, unfortunately! Would you want yours to feel that way? Are they feeling like that right now? Would you dare to ask? Do not fall for the alluring strategic ignorance! For it's never a sustainable or winning one! However, how could you prevent it from happening to your marital partner?

Your destination dictates which route you will take. Isn't it? Likewise, what you want out of your marriage would dictate how you would behave on a daily basis, right? So, constantly use your brain, your common sense! Let it color over your family life. Let it also manage your emotions and feelings, never the other way around. Letting your emotions color over your family's life would surely bring total marital failure, euphemistically called "divorce." You do not want that, right? So please don't leave your 'marriage success' to chance. Don't let external factors such as other people, the media, and the pressures of daily living control what's happening within the walls of your place. Therefore, both partners will have to take deliberate actions to bring about the desired outcome.

"*Noli equi dentes inspicere donati.*" It simply means that looking at a gifted horse in the mouth is never wise. Instead, focus on the horse's strengths, prissy beauty, potential, and usefulness. Likewise, once you take in a new wife, that's it. It should become too late to compare her with others in a negative way. It really never helps in anything useful. Rather, take exquisite pleasure in her, her own beauty, her good qualities, her potential. And she should do the same for you. Strive to keep treating each other like you did during your engagement period. You remember! And you both will be enough for each other in a lifetime!

Always dress up your intentions.

Stay in top shape; that means remaining your husband's 'ish·shah'. Then, a reasonable man will never need your shape. But he will never satisfy … of the female in you like you won't ever get enough of the man in him! For all the same.

Speak up your soul!

Caring for a baby could sometimes be frustrating, but not for lack of love. Instead, it occurred when a caring parent couldn't decipher their intentions or needs behind their random cries or wailings. Thank God that we have brains! But remember, none of us can read minds or hearts! So, use them liberally. Just like this wife who became blind and finally reminded his neglectful husband that nothing, except her eyesight, has changed! So help your partner to help you! Tell each other what you want! Let him/her know your aspirations, fantasies, thoughts, ideas, feelings, emotions, what you want, when, how, how much, and where you want "it" or whatever...etc. "Friendship is a masterpiece of human nature." Offer yours to your partner generously!

Those known unknowns.

Attention! Be frank! From time to time, you may want to find out if they have any intimate fantasies. Then, be willing to be "that person" or do "that thing," evidently considering each other's conscience.

Be femininely creative and innovative in being both "properly and figuratively mild!"

Willingly make yourself intimate and emotionally enough for your partner. But be willing to share your partner's time with his friends. He needs more than you, in order to strive and remain a rounded individual! Then you would have a happy camper getting the best of both worlds!

An experienced and kind-hearted woman once shared a clever insight: the key to capturing a man's attention lies in satisfying his other brain needs! So, continually push the boundaries of his pleasure and excitement! For instance, imagine your man or woman returning home after being away. What's your next move? You might suggest a relaxing bath for him/her or indulge in some playful bathing together, even if you've just showered! And always remember, the more you give to him, the more you'll receive in return!

To keep the excitement alive, surprise him with spontaneous, pantyless moments at home. Slip a "stuff" into his hand or secretly tuck it into his pocket. Then, in an intimate moment, lean in close and tease him with a whisper: "Guess what? I'm not wearing any." These playful surprises can ignite passion and keep the spark alive in your relationship.

After the honeymoon, it's essential to continue treating each other with the same love and care you did back when you were engaged. Keep being sweet, both in your actions and your words. Communication is key – talk to your partner openly and honestly. They'll appreciate knowing your expectations and preferences. Remember to embrace your gender roles. For men, this might mean being supportive and attentive to your partner's needs. And for women, it could mean nurturing your relationship and expressing your femininity. Don't forget to pay attention to the world around you, too. Stay aware of what's happening and who's around so you can navigate life's challenges together. You'll create a strong bond that can weather any storm by nourishing your relationship and staying true to yourselves.

"Having an awareness of the existence of pleasure changes everything!" A burning expectation of it makes humanity always desire to secure "a reliable source" within the matrimonial arrangement. Once such entitlement is created, both partners need to keep feeding the related emotional and intimate interdependence. Indeed, men were made to have a craving for women's bodies and vice versa. They want access to "it"! Your partner knows it; she knows too that you desperately want to be a fellow at "the religion in her hips!" Naturally, she has some rules, though random or rather vain; they are hers! What are you going to do? We're gonna keep singing for our supers, right? For, if each party doesn't keep playing their part reasonably, surely no parachute would be available for anyone after taking the matrimonial jump! So, for your virtual "Husband Wanted" broadcast to be gone off social media once and for all, use mind and body to secure a husband to whom you will always be desired!

_____ The End. _____

www.ingramcontent.com/pod-product-compliance
Lightning Source LLC
Chambersburg PA
CBHW041317110526
44591CB00021B/2812